CONSTELLATIONS

Like the future itself, the imaginative possibilities of science fiction are limitless. And the very development of cinema is inextricably linked to the genre, which, from the earliest depictions of space travel and the robots of silent cinema to the immersive 3D wonders of contemporary blockbusters, has continually pushed at the boundaries. **Constellations** provides a unique opportunity for writers to share their passion for science fiction cinema in a book-length format, each title devoted to a significant film from the genre. Writers place their chosen film in a variety of contexts – generic, institutional, social, historical – enabling **Constellations** to map the terrain of science fiction cinema from the past to the present... and the future.

'This stunning, sharp series of books fills a real need for authoritative, compact studies of key science fiction films. Written in a direct and accessible style by some of the top critics in the field, brilliantly designed, lavishly illustrated and set in a very modern typeface that really shows off the text to best advantage, the volumes in the **Constellations** series promise to set the standard for SF film studies in the 21st century.'
Wheeler Winston Dixon, Ryan Professor of Film Studies, University of Nebraska

 Constellations

Constelbooks

Also available in this series

12 Monkeys Susanne Kord

Blade Runner Sean Redmond

Brainstorm Joseph Maddrey

Children of Men Dan Dinello

Close Encounters of the Third Kind Jon Towlson

The Damned Nick Riddle

Dune Christian McCrea

Ex Machina Joshua Grimm

Inception David Carter

Jurassic Park Paul Bullock

Mad Max Martyn Conterio

RoboCop Omar Ahmed

Rollerball Andrew Nette

Forthcoming

Lost Brigid Cherry

The OA David Sweeney

Seconds Jez Conolly & Emma Westwood

The Stepford Wives Samantha Lindop

CONSTELLATIONS

Stalker

Jon Hoel

Acknowledgements

Gratitude to:

Brett Belcastro, Anna Corbet, Zack Finch, David Langston, Kit Riemer, David Ryan, and Devin Snell.

The poem 'And now summer has left', quoted on p.91 as dialogue from *Stalker*, can be found in *I Burned at the Feast: Selected Poems of Arseny Tarkovsky* (Cleveland State University Poetry Center, 2015).

Thank you so much to Daisy Braun for the gorgeous illustrations. Thank you to John Atkinson for his encouragement and the opportunity. Nostalghia.com is an excellent resource for all things Tarkovsky and I utilized it heavily in my research.

Endless love and gratitude to my family for their support.

First published in 2021 by
Auteur, an imprint of Liverpool University Press,
4 Cambridge Street, Liverpool L69 7ZU
www.liverpooluniversitypress.co.uk/imprints/Auteur/
Copyright © Auteur 2021

Series design: Nikki Hamlett at Cassels Design
Set by Cassels Design www.casselsdesign.co.uk

All rights reserved. No part of this publication may be reproduced in any material form (including photocopying or storing in any medium by electronic means and whether or not transiently or incidentally to some other use of this publication) without the permission of the copyright owner.

British Library Cataloguing-in-Publication Data
A catalogue record for this book is available from the British Library

ISBN paperback: 978-1-9993340-8-6
ISBN hardback: 978-1-80034-833-2
ISBN epub: 978-1-80034-767-0
ISBN PDF: 978-1-80034-562-1

Contents

Roadside Picnic: Introduction ... 7

Pliancy and Weakness (Character Examinations) ... 21

Inside the Zone ... 43

The Aesthetics of *Stalker* ... 65

The Poetics of *Stalker* (Poetic Cinema) ... 89

Afterword ... 99

Films Cited ... 102

Bibliography ... 104

Сталкер *Stalker*

1979 – Mosfilm

Cast:

Alexander Kaidanovsky	'Stalker'
Anatoly Solonitsyn	'Writer'
Nikolai Grinko	'Professor'
Alisa Friendlich	'Stalker's Wife'
Natasha Abramova	'Stalker's Daughter'
Faime Jurno	'Writer's Companion'
Raymo Rendi	'Patrol Police'
E. Kostin,	'Lyuger (Bartender)'

Director: Andrei Tarkovsky

Producers: T. Aleksandrovskaya,, V. Vdovina, M. Mosenkov

Screenplay: Arkady & Boris Strugatsky, Andrei Tarkovsky (not credited).

Cinematography: Aleksandr Knyazhinsky, Leonid Kalashnikov (not credited), Georgy Rerberg (not credited).

Music: Eduard Artemyev

Production Design: Andrei Tarkovsky

Editing: Ludmilla Feiginova

Production Support: Aleksandra Demidova

Production Manager: Larisa Tarkovskaya

Assistant Director: M. Chugunova, Evgeny Tsimbal, Larisa Tarkovskaya

Roadside Picnic: Introduction

'In *Stalker* I make some sort of complete statement: namely that human love is—miraculously—proof against the blunt assertion that there is no hope for the world. That is our common, and incontrovertibility positive possession. Although we no longer quite know how to love.' – Andrei Tarkovsky, *Sculpting in Time*, (1986: 199).

1972: the genesis of *Сталкер* / *Stalker* (1979) begins here, with Soviet brothers, Arkady and Boris Strugatsky, who would collaborate together on an expansive bibliography of science-fiction novels, to great acclaim; most notably a continuous series of books collectively referred to as the 'Noon Universe'. In 1972, they published *пикник на обочине*, (*Piknik na obochine*), an ethereal science-fiction novel, about an alien visitation to Earth, which occurs simultaneously in six different locations on the planet, and the aftermath of that visit. Much of the novel focuses on the character Redrick Schuhart who is a stalker,[1] stalkers being these young rebels who venture into those locations on the planet touched by extra-terrestrial life, called Zones, to retrieve artifacts left by the alien visitors there to sell on the black market. Schuhart is plagued by the mysterious Zone he enters, along with his friend Kirill, a fellow stalker. As their trips to the Zone increase, strange and often tragic misfortunes caused by the strange Zone begin to erupt around them, over the course of the next eight years.

In 1977, after numerous suppressions from Госкомиздат (Goskomizdat), the State Committee for Publishing in the Soviet Union, the book was released in the west, in English, translated by Antonina W. Bouis, and titled *Roadside Picnic*. Upon its American release, in a 1977 DePauw University anthology review, that has since been updated and used as the forward to the novel, fellow science-fiction author Ursula Le Guin called the book: 'Complex in event, imaginative in detail, ethically and intellectually sophisticated, it is, in the last analysis, the story of a particular person, an individual destiny,' and of its authors, 'tender, aware of [their] vulnerability'. In the Soviet Union, the novel mostly appeared in literary publications in the first decade of its existence, with a complete, uncensored version of the book not appearing publicly until the 1990s. But various journals held these slightly abridged versions of the novel, including literary portions of the newspaper *Youth of Estonia* and the literary magazine *Avrora*.

CONSTELLATIONS

Between January 24th and 26th of 1973, while recovering from influenza, Andrei Arsenevich Tarkovsky read the story and immediately saw its potential for adaptation, writing in his diaries: 'I've just read [The Strugatsky Brothers'] science-fiction story, *Roadside Picnic*; that could be a tremendous screenplay for somebody as well' (66). Tarkovsky was friendly with the Strugatsky brothers who he had initially been introduced to in 1971, and would remain friendly with until his death, many years later. Initially, although Tarkovsky was enthusiastic about a filmic interpretation of the novel as he begun to conceive it, he thought his friend, director, and cinematographer Giorgi Kalatozishvili would be a more suitable visionary to direct the project than himself.[2] Kalatozishvili *was* in fact initially interested; but could not obtain the necessary rights to pursue the project and subsequently dropped it.

Tarkovsky was born in a small village called Zavrazhye on April 4th, 1932. He spent most of his formulative years in Yuryevets, a town in the Yuryevetsky District of Ivanovo Oblast, and then later, in Moscow. Initially, he went to university to study Arabic, but dropped out to work as a prospector for the Soviet Academy of Science Institute's Metal and Golds department. Shortly thereafter he decided he would study film.

Tarkovsky's film career began in 1954 while he was still a student studying at the Girasimov Institute of Cinematography in Moscow. While he was there, Tarkovsky directed three short films— *Убийцы/The Killers* (1956), *Сегодня увольнения не будет…/There Will Be No Leave Today* (1957), and *Каток и скрипка/The Steamroller and the Violin* (1961), the last being his Thesis film. Once he graduated from university, Tarkovsky would go on to make seven feature films in total— *Иваново Détство/Ivan's Childhood* (1962), *Андрей Рублёв/Andrei Rublev* (1966), *Солярис/Solaris* (1972), *Зеркало/The Mirror* (1975), *Сталкер/Stalker* (1979), *Nostalghia/Nostalgia* (1983), and *Offret/The Sacrifice* (1986). He also co-directed a documentary about his film theory *Tempo di Viaggio/Voyage in Time* (1983), with his friend, Tonino Guerra, the Italian screenwriter and frequent collaborator of both Fellini and Antonioni. *Stalker* was the fifth, and the last of his films to be made in the Soviet Union; *Nostalghia* (cowritten with Guerra) was an Italian film and *The Sacrifice* was Swedish.

After Kalatozishvili grudgingly passed on the *Roadside Picnic* screenplay, Tarkovsky seemed to start mulling it over more himself: throughout 1973 in his diaries he was planning a film adaptation of Dostoyevsky's *The Idiot*, as well as beginning production on his film *The Mirror*. In his diaries on Christmas he wrote: 'At the moment I can see a film version of something by the Strugatsky brothers as being by a religious action, entirely on the plane of ideas almost transcendental, absurd, absolute' (101), and then again later on: 'What I want is an explosive fusion of the emotional (imbued with the simple, valid feelings of an autobiographical account) with the aspiration to understand certain philosophical and ethical questions which touch on the meaning of life' (101). He met with both Strugatsky Brothers on June 3rd, 1975, received their blessing, and moved forward with the project, beginning pre-production in 1976. As with his first adaptation of a science-fiction novel, Stainslaw Lem's *Solaris*, Tarkovsky was far less interested in creating a loyal translation of the text, then he was with generating his own personal vision—a brand-new interpretation of *Roadside Picnic*. As he worked on the screenplay with the Strugatsky Brothers, they edged further and further from the source material as they worked, evidenced by earlier drafts of the screenplay. Tarkovsky was adept at translating science-fiction to the silver screen, Solaris having been released in 1972 to both critical and commercial accolades.[3]

They had planned to begin shooting after the 26th of January 1977 in what is now Tajikistan, near the city of Isfara there, but an earthquake in nearby Shuraba foiled their filming plans, so instead, Tarkovsky relocated *Stalker* some 4800 kilometers/3000 miles away, to an area outside of Tallinn in Estonia, along the Gulf of Finland, for over a year of shooting there. They had completed about half of their intended shooting there in the summer of 1977, when, upon returning to Moscow, it was discovered by Lyudmila Feyginovay (principal film editor) that all their footage was ruined, likely from poor film-development or because of the quality of the film used, a new Kodak film. Even before this, Tarkovsky's friendship and working relationship with the film's principal cinematographer, Georgy Ivanovich Rerberg had become venomous.

Tarkovsky saw Rerberg as cankerous to the film, and after he saw the disintegrated footage, he seemed vindicated, though he acknowledged that the film's chief engineer, Konoplyov was equally responsible. Estonian director and cinematographer

Arvo Iho—who was a protégé of Tarkovsky's and worked as an intern on the set of *Stalker*—also highlighted Konoplyov as the culprit in an article of an Estonian newspaper in 2011:

> More than 2,000 metres of negatives from Kodak had been developed to a disgusting browny green colour, that was something that Peter Simm and I could see ourselves on the cutting table. This was a new type of Kodak film and Mosfilm's chief engineer, Konoplyov, had 'rationalised', he hadn't purchased a particular chemical, he was saving money. But—looked at another way—if that hadn't happened, we wouldn't have the *Stalker* we now have.

Tarkovsky—understandably—certainly did not see this as an opportunity for improving his film. He was furious, writing in his diaries in August of 1977 that Rerberg had made a mockery of his art, that he was a 'disreputable whore'. He concluded with saying that 'As far as I'm concerned, in other words, he is a corpse' (146). He fired Rerberg and brought on a new cinematographer, Leonid Kalashnikov. Kalashnikov would only work on the project for a couple weeks, before production was halted entirely. When they returned, Kalashnikov refused to work with Tarkovsky, and even used his wife as an intermediary in quitting so he didn't have to speak to the director himself. Shortly thereafter, on April 8th 1978, Tarkovsky had a heart attack. He survived, but was told he would need two months rest to recover, delaying shooting even longer. And, they were out of money. He remarked in his diaries, '*Stalker* is bewitched' (152).

To procure the funds needed for the reshoots, Tarkovsky would tell the Soviet film boards that he now intended to make the film in two-parts, (which, while at the time mostly was an excuse to obtain the funds, would end up becoming true for the film's structure). By the time of its release, *Stalker* would be shot three times in total, the final version working with the cinematographer Alexander Knyazhinsky with whom he was more amiable. Much of the second-filming took place again in Estonia, south of Tallinn, although large portions were also filmed in Dolgoprudny, about 18 miles north of Moscow. There, Tarkovsky, just weeks after his heart attack—against doctor's orders—would shoot most of what would be the third and final version of the film.

Tarkovsky assembled an excellent cast for his film, including his favorite actor, Anatoly Solonitsyn as the Writer. Solonitsyn had worked with Tarkovsky before on *The Mirror* as well as *Solaris* and *Andrei Rublev*. Tarkovsky also cast Nikolai Grinko, another returning actor who had appeared in all of Tarkovsky's films. He cast Alexander Kaidanovsky as the titular Stalker, and Alisa Friendlich as Stalker's Wife. Natasha Abramova would play Stalker's Daughter, Little Monkey. The remaining minor roles in the film would be portrayed by Faime Jurno, Raymo Rendi and E. Kostin. A tiny cast, given the magnitudinal size of the film.

The trio enter the blockade to the Zone. © Mosfilm

There were some noted changes after the first filming—because of budgetary restrictions there were lots of cuts. The primary set editor Rashit Safiullin recalled in a mid-2000s interview with the Criterion Collection that the original version of the film included a dozen tanks and a couple of armored troop carriers to lay abandoned in the misty fields, at the opening of the scene in the Zone where they walk by these vehicle-corpses. But in the re-shoots, they could only budget three tanks and two carriers. Safiullin respected Tarkovsky's drive though, remarking 'With him there had to be not a single unmotivated flower, in the frame, let alone the tanks. We needed an illusion: a great number of tanks being there and like something had happened to them.' The tanks turned out terrifically, with their decay and abandonment appearing very actualized. Additionally, the infamous sequence where the trio burst through the military blockade had virtually no budget. All of the barbed wire and fencing around the track had to be procured by film grips—through various means; Safiullin implies heavily that some of these supplies were stolen—and in the intensity of that scene, you can hardly tell how rickety they are, they look military-grade.

Stalker premiered at the Dom Kino cinema in Moscow on May 14th 1979. Tarkovsky in his diaries expressed hope the film might have premiered at Cannes (250), but the Soviets wanted it shown in Moscow for its opening instead. In total, the film was made with a total approximate budget of ₽3.2 million (approximately $4,896,000 in 1979 USD).[4] The film—upon initial release—was not particularly financially or critically successful. In absentia the fiscal/critical failing makes sense: *Stalker* is an exceptional and unhurried film, which clocks in at just under three hours, and is filled with very long shots—at an average of four minutes per-shot in the film.[5] It lulls you in, with Eduard Artemyev's equally drowsily peaceful and eerily unsettling soundtrack. The film asks a *lot* of you as a viewer, demanding focus and often invoking its visual and mental inquiry—dogged religious imagery darts in and out of shots of the Zone, and while dialogue is sometimes sparse in the film, it is almost always spoken in long, serious soliloquys, with intent and importance. It is an incredibly thoughtful film that pools together philosophies stretching across both cultures and timespans—as ancient as Taoism, and recent as 20th-century contemporaries of Tarkovsky himself. Philosophical echoes of Kierkegaard, Nietzsche, Husserl and Dostoyevsky dart in and out of the film's narrative; the work Stalker does to attempt to bring others to his Zone has been compared to Plato's Allegory of the Cave as a path toward education or enlightenment. Nietzschean interpretative readings of the film can lead it towards far more nihilistic conclusions. Simultaneously, there are enormous political shadows in the film as well; its landscape sharply recalls the Gulags and other psychological confines of life in the USSR, whose censors Tarkovsky constantly battled against until his expatriation.

Emerging into the Zone. © Mosfilm

What is the film about? Famously, the film is so simple to describe, it can be summarized easily, though it is, at its heart, enormously complex. It's partially akin to the plot of the novel though differs largely in tone and specificity. In the simplest terms—and in fact, while the plot is very straightforward it is also an incredibly difficult film to summate in a way that does it justice: an unknown alien entity— presumed to be alien or at least in the abstract—arrived on Earth. According to the intro of the film: '...Was it a meteorite or a visitation from outer space? Whatever it was, in our small country, there appeared a miracle – the ZONE. We sent in troops. Not one returned. Then we surrounded the Zone with a security cordon. We did right...Although I'm not sure...I'm not sure...' The Zone is the fantastical element of a world mostly comprised of realism in the film. It's a mysterious, enigmatic territory known only to the stalkers. The stalkers guide their clientele through the Zone to a mysterious sector within it known as the Room. The Room grants the truest, deepest desires of any person who enters it. Our stalker, known only eponymously as Stalker, lives outside the Zone, with his wife and daughter. He prepares to take his two new clients into the Zone, and meets them at a very filthy bar. Throughout the film, they only acknowledge one another by their occupations: one, the Writer and the other, the Professor. Stalker, Writer, and Professor begin their journey into the Zone, which is guarded on its perimeter by a military blockade. They successfully penetrate this barricade—though they do receive plenty of heavy gunfire—and enter the Zone via a railway car. They begin the treacherous journey to the Room, equal parts physical and metaphysical. The way to the Room is littered with unseen traps and tests; along the way, Stalker preemptively tests new areas by throwing strips of cloth tied to metal nuts, though it is difficult to tell if that does any good. The journey is clearly exhausting to them; they often stop to rest. While the Stalker sleeps along a patch of moss, a black dog trudges up to him in the riverbed and reoccurs for much of the film. The Professor is briefly separated from the other two, when he doubles back for his rucksack. They find him, and he has recovered his rucksack, which he is conspicuously concerned for. They travel on, and the Stalker has them draw lots to see who will go first through the particularly dangerous section of the Zone (the Writer loses the lot, though, it seems fairly obvious that the matches were a grift; Stalker has intended for Writer to go first the whole time. Since the beginning of the journey he seems less certain on Writer as a traveler—when they first begin traveling he encourages Writer to risk himself to find the railway car, before Professor). The second of these is through what is perhaps the film's most famous visual sequence, the Meat Grinder, which takes them through a room filled with small, crescent sand-dunes, called barchans. This leads them to the entrance of the Room, where all three of them in turn refuse to enter. The Professor reveals he has brought in his rucksack a bomb, with which he plans to destroy the Room, so it will not fall into the wrong hands. The Stalker attempts to grab the bomb from him but is easily physically stopped by the other two. This doesn't matter though; the Professor dismantles the bomb himself, having already seemingly decided against it.

In the aftermath of the film's climax, we return to the bar where all three are sitting in silence, the black dog back at the Stalker's feet. Stalker's wife and daughter appear and he and the dog leave with them, trudging along a tiny beachside along a lake and across it, the face of a large nuclear power plant. Back at the apartment, Stalker's

Wife lays out a bowl of milk for the dog. Stalker collapses on the floor, exhausted. His Wife cares for him, helping him into bed. Then the film's finale, a four-minute shot of the Daughter sitting alone at the kitchen table, staring at a glass that autonomously slides itself across the table, presumably by telekinetic means, as an overdub of her voice recites a poem; then the glass falls off the table, does not break, we hear a loud indecipherable collage of western music (apart from Beethoven's *Ninth Symphony*) and the film ends.

The film differs heavily from both the plot and characters featured in *Roadside Picnic*: the novel focuses mainly on the specific stalker Redrick Schuhart and stalkers in general in the novel function more like thieves or raiders as opposed to the film, which sees them more like guides. The novel takes place in Harmont, a fictional town in Canada, certainly a world of difference from the dreary undisclosed Soviet conditions of the film. Tarkovsky takes the film in a firmly philosophical and spiritual direction, as opposed to the more ambiguous mystery of the Strugatskys' original tale.

As noted, in addition to lukewarm financial response upon its initial release, the film was not a success critically either. The Soviet government thought the film was boring and too avant-garde, missing the point entirely. When the film saw a wider release in North America, it was panned as well by mainstream critics in the States. In her review for the *New York Times*, Janet Maslin called the film's style 'stupefyingly drab and slow', complaining about the film's lack of dialogue and finding the final reveal of the mysterious Room in the Zone to be underwhelming in scope (23). Maslin makes reference to the then-recently released *E.T.* (1982) and muses on *Stalker*'s inability to construct such unique fantastical wonderment—which, is pretty ironic, if you consider Spielberg's subsequent descent from promising new director at the start of his career with films like *Jaws* (1975) and *Close Encounters of the Third Kind* (1977) into uneven decades filled with lifelessly unimaginative cookie-cutter films. (I agree with Alex Cox who said that Spielberg became more confectioner than director.) Tarkovsky brushed all these criticisms aside, famously stating: 'I am interested only in the views of two people: one is called Bresson and one called Bergman' (13) He also had keen insight on the quality of the film, remarking to himself in his diaries on February 10th, 1979 before the film's premiere in May that it was his opus:

> I think that *Stalker* really is going to be my best film. That is good to know, but nothing more. Or rather, it makes for greater confidence. It does not for a moment mean that I have a high opinion of my films. I don't like them—there is so much in them that is fussy, ephemeral, false. (Less in *Stalker* than in others.) Which is merely because other people's films are so much worse. Is that pride on my part? Perhaps it is. But it is also the truth (174).

Stalker's pace, most emphatically the first 20-to-30 minutes of the film, is infamously static. When critics from Goskino, the State Committee for Cinematography complained of the film's wearisome starting sequence, Tarkovsky sardonically replied: 'The film needs to be slower and duller at the start so that the viewers who walked into the wrong theatre have time to leave before the main action starts.' His urgency to set the pace of *Stalker* seems somewhat a result of previous experiences:

> I felt it very important that the film observe the three unities of time, space and action...In *Stalker* I wanted there to be no time lapse between the shots. I wanted time and its passing to be revealed, to have their existence, within each frame; for the articulations between the shots to be the continuation of the action and nothing more, to involve no dislocation of time, not to function as a mechanism for selecting and dramatically organizing the material—I wanted it to be as if the whole film had been made in a single shot. Such a simple and ascetic approach seems to me to be rich in possibilities...I wanted the whole composition to be simple and muted (192-193).

The creation of *Stalker* was meticulous and thorough, despite its setbacks. Tarkovsky was a total visionary but difficult to work with for sure. When Eduard Artemyev (who previously worked with Tarkovsky on *Solaris*) was recording the soundtrack for *Stalker*, Tarkovsky refused to be present. When Artemyev asked about this, Tarkovsky bristled remarking that, 'the recording is not a concert'. Admittedly, he backed this up with being some sensible reasoning according to an interview with Artemyev from 2000—that during the recording, he may appreciate music that ends up not suiting the film as a whole image or individual scene, which it was better to decide at the end, once the music was complete. In the interview, Artemyev describes this process as 'being in limbo until the very end, it was horrible'. The musical influence and reach of Artemyev's soundtrack to *Stalker* is ongoing, most notably in the ambient-electronic circles: in the 90s, the popular ambient artist Robert Rich collaborated with another ambient artist, Brian Williams (who records under the name Lustmord), to release a record of ambient music called *Stalker*, based on the soundtrack of the film. The Austin Texas ambient duo Stars of the Lid's 2001 album *The Tired Sounds of Stars of the Lid* featured a sound-clip from the final scene of the film in one of its tracks. There is even a French classical quartet called Tarkovsky Quartet, that have a 11-minute piece called 'Urga' on their 2016 album *Nuit Blanche* which is dedicated to Tarkovsky and derives creatively from both *Stalker* and *Nostalghia*. The superb Japanese electronic-experimental musician Ryuichi Sakamoto released an album called *async* in 2017 that he imagined as the soundtrack to a nonexistent Tarkovsky film. The album is highly insired by both Tarkovsky's art and Artemyev's music, and even includes a sample of David Sylvian, leader singer of the band Japan, reading the poem 'Life, Life' by Arseny Tarkovsky, Andrei's father.

After *Stalker*, Tarkovsky had hoped to make two films—an interpretation of Dostoyevsky's *The Idiot* (a script he had been working on before and during the *Stalker* years, which heavily influenced much of the film), and a film called *The First Day* about the reign of Peter the Great in the 1700s. *The First Day* was to star Natalya Bondarchuk, who had played the role of Hari in *Solaris*. Production was nearing the halfway mark when it was halted by Goskino. They were concerned that the script Tarkovsky was shooting differed significantly from the script he had submitted to them for state approval, mostly in relation to secularism in the USSR. They were demanding reshoots, which infuriated Tarkovsky so much that he abandoned the project. Shortly thereafter he traveled to Italy where he filmed his next project, *Nostalghia* in 1982 and subsequently lost all of his Russian funding entirely. The Soviets went as far as to pressure the Cannes Film Festival into refusing Tarkovsky's *Nostlaghia* receiving the Palme d'Or, arguably the highest achievement in cinema, which it was in competition for, and for which the film had been selected to receive. This prompted Tarkovsky to declare expatriation; he would remain in Europe for the remainder of his life; *Stalker* would be his last Russian film.

He shot his final film, *The Sacrifice* in Sweden in 1985, leading up to what would be the last year of his life. Tarkovsky was suffering from the advance stages of cancer and though he had hoped to still continue working on his adaptation of *The Idiot*, he died, December 29th, 1986. The cancer of the bronchial tubes was of the same/similar strain that killed both his wife Larisa Tarkovskaya, and the actor who played Writer, Anatoly Solonitsyn. It is suspected they may have been badly poisoned, while filming the river scenes, in a riverbank that was polluted with chemicals from a nearby chemical plant. The Tarkovskys are buried together in a Russian emigrant cemetery in a commune in Paris.

Tarkovsky and his films burn radiantly; like a fiery comet crashed into the world of cinema, historic and unprecedented; synonymous with triumphant achievement in film, one of the inescapable greats. Akira Kurosawa, an intellectual contemporary and friend of the man, on occasion of Tarkovsky's death said of him to *Asahi Shimbun Newspaper*: '...His unusual sensitivity is both overwhelming and astounding. It almost reaches a pathological intensity. Probably there is no equal among film directors alive now.' Tarkovsky is unmatched as a filmmaker in many ways, but most admirably so in his ambitious ability to plot unknowable worlds and breathe them to life on the screen. In his all-too-brief career, every picture is bold and precise in every sense, and he never strays from vision, for any reasons. Most so, in *Stalker* the most thoughtful and emotional science-fiction film ever made. A landmark achievement for cinema in the twentieth century, the influence and importance of Tarkovsky in film and in culture is enormous. With an art so complex and cryptic, some audiences would walk away completely mystified by the film's philosophical and physical wanderings.

It's not difficult to see the lasting impact of *Stalker*, in some instances very directly—there's a popular video-game franchise by Ukrainian game developer GSC Game World called *S.T.A.L.K.E.R.* that takes a wide-inspiration from the film (mostly just its landscape and general conception) and uses it for the setting of several violent first-person-shooter games; these games have been widely well-received and developed a cult following. Films as diverse in range as *Forbrydelsens element/The Element of Crime* (1984), *L'intrus/The Intruder* (2004), *District 9* (2009), *Chernobyl Diaries* (2012), *Under the Skin* (2013), *Arrival* (2016), and *Annihilation* (2018) are all indebted to the style and influence of *Stalker*. The success of the film has also seen multiple reprintings of the Strugatsky's novel *Roadside Picnic* which has brought many audiences worldwide to their bibliography for the first time. Most essentially, the film's popularity brought it an exuberant rerelease from the Criterion Collection in 2017, complete with its first full-digital restoration. The atmosphere and aesthetic of a film should always be its most digestible assets and this restoration of *Stalker* amplifies both aspects, cascading them onto screen brilliantly, for a whole new generation of audiences.

Endnotes

1. The term 'stalker' for these men, has an unclear origin. Many fans of Tarkovsky on the internet have theorized it was chosen as an allusion by the Strugatsky brothers to the titular 'Stalky' or Arthur Lionel Corkran of Rudyard Kipling's short story collection *Stalky & Co*, though our working contemporary definition of 'stalker' e.g. 'to stalk ones' prey,' or 'actioning intrusively against a quarry into unwanted territories' is an accurate definition of the profession as surmised as well. The allusion's credibility is unauthenticated, however.
2. There is an enormous amount of misinformation on this initial recommendation to Kalatozishvili. Many texts written about Tarkovsky, claim that he first recommended the film to Kalatozishvili's father, Mikail Kalatozov, who was the director of the Palme d'Or-winning film Летят журавли/*The Cranes Are Flying* (1957) as well as the film Неотправленное письмо/*Letter Never Sent* (1960). This reads as unlikely however, because Kalatozov died of a heart attack on the 27th of March 1973, leaving little time for him to attempt to seek rights for the film, since it was less than two months after Tarkovsky read *Roadside Picnic*. It seems more likely that it was Kalatozishvili; his age and relatively unknown stature at the time makes him far more likely a contemporary of Tarkovsky than Kalatozov. The mistake is understandable, given Kalatozov's name and its familiarity.
3. Critics praised his vision of adaptation for the novel. However, Stanislaw Lem, the Polish author of *Solaris* was dissatisfied with Tarkovsky's adaptation, going as far as to say in a 1989 interview with Polish critic Stanislaw Bereś that Tarkovsky had 'not made [*Solaris*] at all, he made *Crime and Punishment*. What we get in the film is only how this abominable Kelvin has driven poor Hari to suicide. [...] Tarkovsky reminds me of a sergeant from the time of Turgenev [19th century author of *Fathers and Sons* among others] – he is very pleasant and extremely prepossessing and at the same time visionary and elusive. One cannot 'catch' him anywhere because he is always at a slightly different place already. This is simply the type of person he is. When I understood that I stopped bothering.'
4. This figure is an estimate, and the result of the author conferring with a Slavic Studies expert and an economist friend. Previously published estimates of the budget vary wildly, but the author believes this to be as accurate an estimate as possible, given the

dramatically fluctuating conversion rates at the time. Inflated to 2020 rates, the USD budget is around $17 million.
5. Average estimate comes from Vida Johnson in her book *The Films of Andrei Tarkovsky, a Visual Fugue* written with Graham Petrie.

Pliancy and Weakness (Character Examinations)

'When a man is born, he is soft and pliable. When he dies, he is strong and hard. When a tree is growing, it's tender and pliant. But when it's dry and hard, it dies. Hardness and strength are death's companions. Flexibility and softness are the embodiment of the freshness of life. That which has become hard shall never triumph.' – The Stalker (*Stalker*, 1979)

© Daisy Braun

Stalker, at its heart, is an interplay of unknowable themes and complex characters interacting within a psychic and realized landscape. As a film, it is more driven by its profoundly human protagonists than its more quotidian science-fiction elements: three men walking tenaciously from point A to point B to experience something immaterial. Tarkovsky himself acknowledges this, in response to criticisms that his 'science-fiction art film' was lacking in the science-fiction department:

In *Stalker* only the basic situation could strictly be called fantastic. It was convenient because it helped to delineate the central moral conflict of the film more starkly. But in terms of what actually happens to the characters, there is no element of fantasy. The film was intended to make the audience feel that it was all happening here and now, that the Zone is there beside us (200).

The Zone is most attractive to us—it's the shiny object of the film, begging for analysis. But really, *the heart* of the heart of the film, is its characters. For the moment at least, let's stay with them. We spend most of the film with three men traveling to/in the Zone: The Writer, the Professor and the Stalker, who leads the other two there.

The scene where the characters are first available to us completely, as both entirely fallible and vulnerable, is the longshot when they are first entering the Zone. The soldiers who defend the barricade open fire on the men, who get through unharmed, though narrowly. They abandon their vehicle in exchange for a much smaller railcar. The Stalker calmly warns the other two: 'If anyone's hit, don't cry out, do not fuss: if they spot you, they'll kill you... Then when everything's quiet crawl back to the post. You'll be picked up later.' We already had a sense of the specialness of the Zone, but the way in which Stalker quietly—but urgently—mutters this warning is the moment we begin to feel the vulnerability of all three men: they are, and will remain, in danger, for the rest of their journey. The men are constantly wincing, their movements for the most part, steadily lethargic. They stop to rest often, which leaves them very available to us for dissecting. Few films successfully manage to highlight characters with this level of complexity, while simultaneously never neglecting their non-character-centric plot and atmosphere. *Stalker* engages its characters with the goal of demonstrating the wonderment and winsome aspects of humanity and dignity, that's what Tarkovsky is striving for most of the time with the three men in the film, toying with that dignity, its removal—and consequentially—depravity and renewal. While each man seems to come to the Zone with their individual sense of purpose and intentionality, the homogenous quality among the three is their disillusionment or, rather, disenchantment, with the exterior world. The unsatisfactory quality of their lives (the two clients, and Stalker as well) leads them to narratively ill-advised venture into the Zone, something that ordinary people seem not keen to pursue, in the world of the film.

Professor

The Professor (or the Scientist as he is sometimes referenced), takes a more analytical approach to the psychological journey to the Room. As noted, he is a scientist and, as we discover, has come along on the journey with the ultimate intent to destroy the Room, with a bomb concealed in his rucksack. When we first encounter Professor, it becomes clear that he operates in certain contrast to both Writer and Stalker, both of whom seem to come to things from an emotion-driven place, most of the time, in most circumstances we encounter. The Professor though, tries to maintain a scientific perspective. He's a scientist—a physicist specifically, and initially dodges questions as to what his reasoning is for the journey into the Zone. Eventually we find out his precise rationale for blowing up the room: '...One should never perform irreversible actions. I understand that, I'm not a mania. But so long as this canker is open for every scoundrel...there can be no rest. But maybe something inside us won't permit it?' By the time they arrive, he seems considerably less certain about his task, perhaps now truly believing that the innermost of the Room *will not* allow that cancerous invasion of itself or otherwise, has come to the conclusion that perhaps the Room is in fact fatuous, and after a brief tussle with Stalker it's not long before he dismantles the bomb. For the Professor, perhaps even more so than the other two, for whom the 'moment' of the Room seems almost essential, the *journey* rather than the destination is paramount.

Likely due to the scientific nature *of* science-fiction films, there is a large amount of them that do include these cold, mission-oriented scientist types in central roles in their plots, as sensible inclusions in missions that, such as the one in *Stalker*, would probably naturally occur, and induce their interests because of personality traits or occupational obligations. In Danny Boyle's film *Sunshine* (2007) the protagonist Robert Capa, is an emotionally-detached, mostly silent physicist on board a suicide-mission in a spaceship called *Icarus II* headed to reignite a dying sun. Capa portrays the mannerisms of a physicist under those circumstances execratorially. Like the Professor in *Stalker*, Capa truly understands the magnitude of their mission, its implications for humankind, and of the power of his spaceship's payload—a 'starbomb'—which easily explains his emotional introversion. Likewise, the actions and mindset of the Professor in the Zone are classifiable by his expected conclusion of blowing up the Room. When they first arrive in this section of the Zone, there is a mysterious and absurd telephone there, that is distinct in its existence in the film, for two reasons—there shouldn't *be* an operating phone in the middle of the Zone, which is defunct of telephone lines, or anything that could properly feed electricity, and the fact that it rings at this precise moment, obviously. It's not particularly clear if the phone *is* real or not, if it's imagined or if it's a fantastical thing, that is supposed to be taken very literally. Either way, it functions somewhat the same. The best we can surmise is that it *is* real, because of the scene where Writer cuts at the electric wires with his knife, giving the telephone as a reason. When the Professor picks up the phone, he communicates with people from his laboratory—the ninth one, we are told. The person on the other end of the phone communicates all kinds of vital information to us: that (according to the voice) all Professor has ever wanted is to do harm, that he is, at least in part, setting off the bomb in response to the voice's having slept with the Professor's wife, some twenty years prior. He also compares the Professor to Herostratus, the Greek arsonist who burned down the Temple of Artemis. After he hangs up on the voice, the Writer asks him what this was all about. Instead of answering him, the Professor seems to be weighing the importance of destroying the Room now, saying:

> Imagine what will happen when everyone believes in this Room...and when they all come hurrying here. It's only a question of time. Not today, but tomorrow. And in the thousands. All these would-be-emperors, grand inquisitors, fuhrers of all shades. The so-called saviors of mankind. And not for money or inspiration, but to remake the world!

At this point at least, he seems resolved to still go through with things, though he is perhaps still only interested in the proclamation of destroying the Room, more than in the actual act itself.

Why then does he not do so? It is possible that simply declaring his intention to fulfill the dangerous mission, in spite of the outry of his academic/laboratory's community, and completing the physical portion of the pilgrimage to the room, was enough for him. After the three men have tussled over the bomb and Stalker lays weeping, Writer has voiced some serious doubts as to whether the Room actually has any

Professor explaining his intention to blow up The Room. © Mosfilm

wondrous element at all:

> That which comes true here is that which reflects the essence of your true nature. It is within you. It governs you. Yet you are ignorant of it. It sits in you and rules your life. [...] I will not go into your Room. I do not want to pour all the filth in my soul on anybody's head – even yours. [...] I'd rather drink myself to death and stay grunting in my stinking private villa. No, you're a bad judge of human nature if you bring people like me into the Zone. [...] How did you learn, that this miracle really exists? [To Professor] Who told you that desires really come true here? Do you know one man who made happy here? Perhaps Porcupine?

After this monologue, Professor wordlessly dismantles his bomb, defeatedly. Is this because he no longer believes in the Room? More likely he interprets Writer's description of the *essence* of you, being what desire, the Room fulfills, in relation to Porcupine's fate—massive wealth—as opposed to his desired outcome from the room;

the resurrection of his dead brother. Professor realizes there isn't a need to destroy the Room under its true conditions. Though, as said, it's likely he was never actually going to destroy the Room at all. He sits down with Writer and Stalker casting the various bits and plates of the bomb into the water. He utters his final line of the film: 'I do not understand anything at all. What's the sense in coming here?' Stalker muses on the idea of moving to the Zone with his wife and daughter so nobody will ever hurt them. Professor finishes tossing the dismantled bomb into the water and the film fades away, back into a monochromic coloring and back to the outside of the Zone for the remainder of the film.

The Professor is played by Nikolai Grinko, another frequent collaborator of Tarkovsky's—he had a leading or supporting role in every Tarkovsky film from *Ivan's Childhood* to *Stalker*, notably playing Kelvin's Father in *Solaris* and Daniil Chorny in *Andrei Rublev*. In addition to his work with Tarkovsky, he had supporting roles in dozens of other films in his career, none of these being as noteworthy as his work with Tarkovsky, with the exception perhaps to Sergei Parajanov's excellent film *Тіні забутих предків/Shadows of Forgotten Ancestors* (1965).

Writer

The Writer is, perhaps, the most interesting character of the three in the film. His mood can be jovial and lightly humored, but he is also jeering, cold and cynical. He (according to Tarkovsky) '...sets out for the Zone in order to encounter the Unknown, in order to be astonished and startled by it. In the end, however, it is simply a woman [Stalker's Wife] who startles him by his faithfulness and by the strength of her human dignity' (199). When we first meet the Writer in the film however, he's lamenting to his own female companion about the mundanity of life. It is clear he is taking the upcoming journey to the Zone rather cynically, though simultaneously is going on this adventure because he craves something more, likely to influence his writing. When they greet Stalker, he coldly refuses the accompaniment of the lady—it is unclear why. Potentially because of her gender, because she didn't pay for voyage, because he specifically had expected two companions already, it is unknown. What we do witness is the Writer who goes from semi-intoxicated babbling about how she will be accompanying them, to a clear indifference at her departure. He is apparent to us as an apathetic person, bored, alcoholic, irritated.

Our first decipherable anecdote he gives us is when the Writer, Stalker and Professor are having a drink before they begin their journey into the Zone. Writer describes to them an antique pot, a chamber pot that a jester purposefully slips to archeologists curating work for the museum. The fake goes unnoticed and is among the correct pieces, receiving equal praise from connoisseurs. He is perhaps recalling a famous incident where there was an attempted inclusion of a piece of avant-garde art called *Fountain*, a urinal signed R. Mutt made by Dadaist Marcel Duchamp for an exhibition by the Soviet of Independent Artists in 1917. The significant change here is, unlike the pot Writer describes, *Fountain* was ultimately rejected from that exhibition, but then went on to receive wide acclaim and various reproductions in the following decades. The pot is included and even cherished as if it were an artifact in the collection. This could also be directly alluding to the plot of *Roadside Picnic* where stalkers steal such objects from the Zone, believing them to be supernatural. Writer's choice in recounting this gives us an indication of Writer's sense of cynicism with the sociological world he inhabits, for sure. He is more irritated with these ready-made art accolades than with the thing itself, an impatient dismissal of the tongue-in-cheek surrealist sublimity. The notion of historicity infuriates him, perhaps because of his sense of impermanence. The Writer is an objectivist, as evidenced by his displeasure with postmodern sublimities. He's cynical always, openly mocks the faith-work of Stalker as shrewd, a hoax. After the scene with the telephone, the Writer confronts the Stalker as the Professor is leaving the room with the phone:

> ...By the way, I can see that all this poetry reciting [Stalker has just recited the poem from Porcupine's brother, 'And now summer has left' to the other two] and walking around in circles is nothing but a new, original way of apologizing. I understand you. A difficult childhood, social environment...But don't you fool yourself. [Writer puts on a branch of wire on his head, as a makeshift crown of thorns] I, don't forgive you.

Writer feels he has uncovered that the Room, and perhaps the whole Zone is a big grift. He both acknowledges that to Stalker, that he thinks he knows what he is doing and is certainly not going to forgive him for it. The Writer is very distrusting of Stalker, and taunts him throughout their journey, mocking his faith and referring to him mockingly as 'Chingachgook', an allusion to the eponymous character of James Fenimore Cooper's novel *Last of the Mohicans*, a hunter and guide to the young English Munro sisters. It's an insult because Stalker seems to stumble on the details of the Zone occasionally. When Writer first uses this nickname to Professor, it's more candid, less venomous: 'I had imagined stalkers to be different [...] Like Leatherstocking, [another Cooper character] or Chingachgook or Big Serpent.' To which the Professor replies: 'Our Stalker's biography is more terrifying. He was in prison several times, and he was crippled here. His daughter is a mutant, a so-called Zone victim. They say she has no legs.' The truth seems to lie somewhere in the middle—Stalker is battle-weary, physically suffering from having spent too much time in the possibly-radiated borders of the Zone (we know from his exchanges with his Wife that he has been to prison). But much of Writer's cynicism towards Stalker continues throughout the duration of their journey. As mentioned he asserts near the end of their journey that, now, he understands Stalker. He sees the man as a fraud, a profiteer who perhaps leads desperate men to this 'Holy Room' that begets their inner wishes. Regardless of if the Room is real or not, it doesn't matter to Writer, because (a) if it is not real, it's all a sham, and (b) if it is real, it's a matter of trembling with faith and since it likely won't result with the desires you seek anyway, what does it matter? Especially if, like Porcupine your true innermost desire is so unwholesome and foul. He seems resolute at this point, though for just a moment, when they reach the Room, he does seem to hesitate; perhaps he *could* believe. But only for a moment, when Stalker addresses him he immediately withdraws and refuses to enter. Writer seems aware of a fatal flaw in the Room as it is unlikely one would be able to conjure their conception of the desire, and he seems bitterly resolute in tormenting Stalker after they struggle over Professor's bomb.

Like the Professor who has brought along his bomb, Writer has a weapon as well; before exiting the Meat Grinder, he takes out a pistol, to the instant dismay of Stalker who insists if he does not immediately disarm the Zone will kill him for it.

Writer just after leaving the Zone. © Mosfilm

It's unknown how serious this claim might be, more likely it seems as if something Stalker is saying just to get him to disarm himself, but either way, he obliges, tossing the gun aside—Stalker firmly slides it further into the murky water when he and Professor catch up to that spot in the Meat Grinder. Shortly thereafter comes the most important moment in the film for Writer's character. After the ordeal of the Meat Grinder, which genuinely seems to take a huge toll on his character, they come to the room with the sand dunes, which sees the trio all hit the ground fast, in anticipation of some kind of booby-trap or repercussion for disobedience; Writer was supposed to wait at the entrance outside the door of the Meat Grinder and instead moved forward through the dunes. After they all go prone, we see a bird fly through to the same spot in the room twice. Writer loses his nerve for a moment afterwards, and breaks into a soliloquy, staring off into the distance and then, into the camera directly:

> Here you have ... one more experiment. Experiments, fact or truth as a last resort. But there's no such thing as facts, especially here. All this is someone's idiotic

invention. Can't you tell? You, of course, want to know whose invention. What good will it do you to know? Whose conscience will be bothered by it? Mine? I have no conscience, only nerves. Some bastard abuses you, you're hurt. A different bastard praises you, you're hurt. You put your heart and soul into your work and they devour you. Then even devour the filth in your soul. They're all literate. They all have voracious appetites. They all keep crowding round – journalists, editors, critics, a constant stream of women. All of them clamoring for more. What kind of writer am I...if I detest writing? If it's torture for me, a painful, shameful occupation something akin to extruding hemorrhoids. I used to think my books helped some people to become better, but nobody needs me. If I die, in a couple days, they'll find someone else to devour. I wanted to change then, but they've changed me to fit their own image. Once, the future was only a continuation of the present. All its changes loomed somewhere beyond the horizon. But now the future's a part of the present. Are they prepared for this? They don't want anything. They only devour!

Here we have Writer unwound. Throughout the various moments of the film, we get more Writer than anyone else; he's very talkative and his character operates behind various ambiguities, we can't be certain when he's being direct with us and when he's not. But here, Writer has certainly lost his nerve, all guises are down—he is unveiling his true feelings about himself, as an artist, as well as his mortality and fear of immanentism and permanence. Stalker and Professor's personal and moral dilemmas can feel more subjugated to us as an audience, whereas Writer's feels very direct and empathetic to us. He is a man caught in the unbearable banality of regular life, of mediocrity in his art, and presumably, his personal life as well. If Stalker, is representative of the best qualities of human dignity, true faith and morality, then Writer certainly stands in for intellectual nihilism, uncertainty and questioning. When he begins speaking of the future-becomes-present, it's clear that whatever answers he was hoping to find from the Room are lost to him, if the Room is real, he will be unable to ascertain what it is he wants. He is bitterly aware of his own fleeting immanence.

The Writer can sometimes feel a secondary character to Stalker himself, but one might also feel the weight of the story often comes from Writer's perspective, as opposed to Stalker's. Tarkovsky clearly recognized how difficult and important the character would be, since he cast his favorite actor, Anatoly Solonitsyn in the role. Solonitsyn was certainly Tarkovsky's most important collaborator in his films and an excellent actor in his own right, of extreme talents—he played Andrei Rublev in the film of the same name, Dr. Sartorious in *Solaris*, multiple roles in *The Mirror*, the titular author, in the biopic Двадцать шесть дней из жизни Достоевского/*Twenty Six Days from the Life of Fyodor Dostoyevsky* (1981), among other films. According to his diaries, Tarkosky had intended for Solonitsyn to play the lead role of Andrei Gorchakov in his penultimate film *Nostalghia*, but unfortunately Solonitsyn died in the film's preproduction.

Stalker

The Stalker, unsurprisingly (he is titular, after all) is the most-developed character throughout the film, and along with Writer, most complex perhaps, of all its subjects. Tarkovsky was reading and blueprinting his adaptation of *The Idiot* at the time he was beginning to envision *Stalker*, and there are definitive comparisons to be drawn between Stalker himself and Myshkin, the protagonist of Dostoyevsky's book (insofar as they interact spiritually within their respective narratives). Both men share a gentleness, an endearing naiveté, and, consequentially, narratives divulged from those traits. Stalker, like Myshkin is faith-bound almost to a fault, a simple Manichaeism of sorts, categorical ideas of good and evil and obsession with dignity. Stalker is burdened, weary from his previous excursions into the Zone. He is deeply traumatized but steadfast: 'The Stalker seems to be weak,' wrote Tarkovsky on his protagonist, 'But essentially it is he who is invincible because of his faith and his will to serve others' (181). When we first meet Stalker, in the opening of the film, it becomes clear he is driven by his belief system. His Wife pleads with him not to return to the Zone, but he brushes her off. The most telling line of dialogue from this interaction comes from his response to her insistence that he will fail on his journey into the Zone and, in all likelihood, end up back in prison: 'God the Prison! I'm imprisoned everywhere. Let me go. Let me go!' The Stalker is bound by his faith to remain the guide for those seeking the Room, he firmly believes in this servitude. The despair in the man becomes clearer as we move with him throughout the film, but even in this opening sequence it's quite easy to see how troubled he is. At one time, in his outlining, Tarkovsky had planned a much darker turn for Stalker's character: in a conceptualized sequel film, we would have seen Stalker as a neofascist, an older, embittered man, forcibly dragging unwilling individuals through the Zone into the Room, tyrannizing them into happiness. It's good this film was never made—an overly simplistic indoctrination of a more literal plot involving the Room, simply would not work. Nor—I think—would a darker, fully-broken version of Stalker's character be very appealing as a viewer. It is Stalker's humanity, his gentle gait, like Myshkin, that makes his character the ideal entry point and guide for the story. We can make Christlike comparisons with Stalker—as well as Myshkin of course—but perhaps a better reading of the character is to consider him as someone who displays Christlike behaviors on occasion, but is also occasionally fallible and distinctly selfish; his supposed disobedience in entering the Room for his daughter. The Stalker for Tarkovsky—like Dostoyevsky's Prince Myshkin, is an attempt to achieve a character who is utterly Christlike, an extremist in their devotion to the idol of their faith, but who can only inevitably becomes destroyed by the inhumanities around them, goes mad because of them, too gentle for the harshness of the actual world.

The work Tarkovsky does by giving us the Stalker's rationale for who he brings into the Zone is really admirable, there would be easier, lazier, methods of communicating the same task: consider *The Matrix* (1999)—forgetting for a moment what The Matrix itself actually is, and thinking of it instead in Kierkegaardian terms as an 'existential sphere' where a person must temporarily suspect any idea of ethical absolution for an absurd religious moment (think Abraham killing Isaac, or as Walter Benjamin did, consider it as an ahistoric moment suspended entirely from any linear historicism). Morpheus then, is The Stalker of the Matrix, burdened by the carceral nature of being the guide/being subservient to this ineffable 'thing', the only lightening of the burden is the strengthening of his belief, his faith. That's why he so easily sacrifices himself for Neo, it's his faith-based moment. The Wachowskis, who are excellent filmmakers in many other ways, do take the easier approach with this aspect of *The Matrix*. Neo and others are simply 'chosen', they have an unnamed predisposition in their character(s) to be 'awakened' by Morpheus, i.e. taking the journey to the Zone/

A close up of Stalker. © Mosfilm

awakened into the Real World of the Matrix. Not only does *Stalker* assert itself by reasoning with us, with Stalker explaining his decision to bring these characters—or any—to the Zone, we also require and are semi-satisfyingly given explanation from both the Writer and the Professor on their decision to be taken there. It's difficult work to do this, but in the end leads to a more satisfying emotional journey with these characters, who we have some grounded understanding of.

Kurosawa (a noted contemporary of Tarkovsky who wrote an excellent essay about visiting him during the filming of *Solaris*) is an excellent precedent on establishing believable and fascinating reasons for the actions of his characters. Often in his films, characters behave in ways that are distinctly contradictory to what is initially setup as the established belief systems. Kurosawa, like Tarkovsky never blatantly spells out the reasons for these choices, but does always infer them, in some way or another. The juxtaposition of a character's set beliefs/ethics and then circumvents expected conclusion or action of that character for enjoyable storytelling. This might sound somewhat elementary for narrative in cinema; but consider how many films don't bother with building the complexity of the psyche of its characters. Tarkovsky and Kurosawa both build their characters up, and break them down, focusing on bringing raw unnerving emotionality to life on the screen. The juxtaposition of characters in *Stalker* with their varying points of perceiving the reality or false-realities of the Zone—while not to the degree of the 'retellings'—is at least conducted to the tune of Kurosawa's 羅生門/*Rashomon* (1955). *Rashomon* is the film that widely introduced unreliable narration to cinema on a worldwide scale, and Stalker himself certainly checks all of the boxes to qualify as an unreliable narrator himself. In literature, we acknowledge a modernist text to be determined by its dominant force, the epistemology. We can see this turn to unreliable narration as casting structural epistemological doubt in the viewer, and perceive this through the metalingual skepticism in the dialogue. Returning to *Rashomon*: we have a film with three initial accounts of the same event, all of which are proven to be false in at least some way. The narrations are told in greedy self-interest and directly conflict. When we get the truest account from the Woodcutter, even the final version is marred by its self-interest and potential inconsistencies. The uncertainty of the plot and the unreliability of its narrators gives the film a lot more intrigue to contemplate. With *Stalker* and the Stalker, it's a little more complex: we don't know if the Stalker is unreliable. To some extent we have to take it on faith that he truly believes everything he says and has experienced. While at times, Writer and Professor certainly think he's grifting them, it's difficult to come away with that opinion—Stalker's faith seems deeply embedded within him, it would be very difficult to attempt to label him as duplicitous.

The character of Stalker is portrayed by Alexander Kaidanovsky. Unlike Solonitsyn as Writer and Grinko as Professor, who were both returning collaborators, *Stalker* was his first, and only collaboration with Tarkovsky. Kaidanovsky also starred in the film *Свой среди чужих, чужой среди своих*/*At Home Among Strangers* (1975) directed by Nikita Mikhalkov, which also featured Solonitsyn in a lead role. Kaidanovsky and Solonitsyn also collaborated on the film *Телохранитель*/*The Bodyguard* (1979) directed by Ali Khamraev, which was Solonitsyn's last film before his death in 1982. Tarkovsky seemed excited to work with Kaidanovsky, and although Solonitsyn was his favorite actor, he cast Kaidanovsky as the lead.

The character of Stalker's Wife is played by Alisa Freindlich who shows an impressive range of emotions without even saying all that much in the film. While the beginning of the film displays her as one-dimensional, the overly-hysterical spouse—cringingly so—the latter half of the second part of the film features her more refined, interesting and multi-dimensional. Freindlich—who has appeared in dozens and dozens of films, including Простая смерть/*A Simple Death* (1985) a thrilling adaptation of Tolstoy's *The Death of Ivan Illyich*—is an ideal candidate for the role, though originally Tarkovsky had actually intended to cast his wife Larisa Tarkovskaya in the role; she had portrayed Alexei's neighbor Nadezhda in Tarkovsky's previous film *The Mirror*, but he was persuaded to utilize Freindlich instead. A failing of further development into the character of the Wife herself, the relationship cast between the burdened Stalker and his blindly-devoted spouse is the more intriguing concept in the film.

Stalker and his wife's relationship is not so different, and perhaps even spiritually inspired by the relationship between Inga Landgré's character Karin opposite Max Von Syow's Antonius Block in Bergman's classic film *Det sjunde inseglet/The Seventh Seal*. Like the Wife in *Stalker*, Karin is barely featured in the film at all, only making her appearance at the very end of the film, where she is revealed as having been dutifully awaiting Block's return at their castle, in spite of all its other occupants fleeing from an unnamed plague, presumably the Black Death which is manifested in the film as a literal Death incarnate, played by Bengt Ekerot. Karin and Block enjoy one last final supper together before Death comes for them. Bergman's film, like *Stalker*, toils with the heaviest of themes imaginable and a lot of its thematic centricity relates back to these same ideas of human dignity, and the dignity between its characters. The similarities between Block and Stalker continue further: both *Stalker* and *The Seventh Seal* are films about traversing geography, that invariably shifts into a faith-based dilemma, looking inward, and back again into a world of absolution and didactics. Scholar Phoebe Pua in her essay on Tarkovsky and Bergman notes: 'The journey motif in *Stalker* exteriorizes an interior question for true faith, as in *The Seventh Seal*. [...] Though *Stalker*'s characters do not question the existence of God and the relevance of faith in the verbally direct way that Antonius does, the film is as engaged with the discussion of the Great Silence as *The Seventh Seal*' (68). Unlike Antonius Block, Stalker does not seem to falter in his religious

Stalker's Wife, played by Alisa Freindlich. © Mosfilm

faith, but by the end of the film he certainly seems utterly discouraged in his faith in humanity, in their capacity for true faith, as he conceptualizes it, and he does so as an inherent necessity for the continued survival of people, so of course, this conclusion throws him into utter despair, at the end of the film.

The tender, intimate moments between Stalker and his Wife at the end of the film are certainly some of the most compelling in the film, and also highly illuminating of his character and further, his relationship with the Zone. The journey—emotionally, physically, perhaps metaphysically—has taken such a toll on the man that he can barely stagger into his bed, removing his clothing seems to take enormous effort. He seems quite brutalized by the attitudes of Writer and Professor from the Room. He bemoans the 'intelligentsia', the academics and their inability to conceptualize the level of faith he finds necessary to acquiesce into the Room. Interestingly, right before this, we see their apartment is overflowing with books, they're littered against a wall, hundreds of books, impressing upon us that Stalker himself is no fool, or at least, a well-read one. The frustrations we observe him experiencing, the agony, at the end of the film are pretty weighted since we know how hard he pushed Writer and Professor to accept the Room. The dreary fascist future Tarkovsky mused on for a potential sequel feels totally poignant in these final scenes of *Stalker*—fascism doesn't seem like much of a stretch for the man of faith, so tortured by his companions' failures to engage in the manner he finds most amiable. If *Stalker* is ultimately a film about human dignity, then the subsequent removal of that dignity would render his character confusing and upsetting. A person reveals themselves completely only when thrown out of the customary conditions of their life, for only then do they have to fall back on their reserves. If we are to treat Stalker like Prince Myshkin, as infallibly pure and naïve, then the future turn to fascism seems even more cruel and squeamishly unsatisfying as an audience. Which, ultimately, may be why Tarkovsky did not pursue a sequel film.

Tarkovsky's Great Failing

One would be remiss to not address a lingering criticism of Tarkovsky and of *Stalker*: the problematic and dimensionally uninteresting domesticity of Stalker's Wife and then, at large, Tarkovsky's women characters in his films. While she is profoundly loyal to him and shows this in ways that are extremely essential to the final developments of Stalker's character and the plot itself, his Wife as a character is given very little in terms of an 'arc' and lies mostly abandoned in the foreground for most of the film. Literally, Stalker leaves her weeping and writhing on the floor of their kitchen, in the opening of the film, an overly and unnecessarily sexualized expression of grief—while she writhes, her nipples are shown pressing through her blouse and there is a kind of rising climax to the grief. It is a scene that should perhaps be seen with an amount of exasperation. She's always seen as obsessing over her husband, a doting spouse. And it's not as if Tarkovsky is incapable of writing provocative female characters—most strongly evidenced by excellent characters written and shot for his films *The Mirror* and *Solaris*—which makes it all-the-more squeamish to see such a disinterest here. A feminist reading of *Stalker* is not complimentary; while the plot is terrific, delving into the wondrous human psyche of its characters, it's inexorably limited with its sole focus on the male psyche. When Stalker's Wife begs him to allow their daughter and she to come live with him in the Zone, an act *he himself* was contemplating mere scenes before, he sternly refuses, despite his weary bedridden condition. Tarkovsky himself is troublingly sexist at times, most upsettingly in an infamous interview with the Slovakian-Swedish journalist Irena Brežná, in March of 1984 for the Berlin magazine *Tip*.

The troubling article showcases a brazen and defensive Tarkovsky. Brežna tells Tarkovsky that, while she is touched by his films, she cannot find herself in them; that women are only portrayed through the male gaze. She charges that his female characters seem to only exist to revolve around their relationships with men. Tarkovsky responds: 'I have never thought about that, I mean about the woman's interior world. It would be difficult to deny the woman her own world, but it seems to me that this world is very strongly connected to the world of the man that the woman is involved with. From this point of view, a solitary woman is an abnormality' (106). He goes on to say women and men who do not 'dissolve' into one another in a relationship, often turn cold. He goes as far as to tell Brežná that she is not content with her own female nature (111). He has brief redemptive moments in the interview—acknowledging an urgent need for social equalities for women, saying he is *for* this, some brief but well-worded critiques of Thatcherism, and a general attempt to focus on more on valuing spirituality above immanence, but it's all minor points in contrast to the wince-inducing statements like: 'the meaning of female love is self-sacrifice'. The interviewer does acknowledge an admiration for Tarkovsky's filmic basic human condition in *Stalker* and *Solaris*, highlighting the way he portrays love in *Solaris*, through Hari and Kelvin.

Tarkovsky's worst sexism comes from his film after *Stalker, Nostalghia* which, while visually and narratively breathtaking, is almost unbearable in its tone-deaf depictions of women, objectional and amateurish, far in contrast to some of his more viably inoffensive depictions of women. *Nostalghia* comes after the best period of Tarkovsky's filmography: 1966-1979, with *Andrei Rublev, Solaris, The Mirror*, and *Stalker*. These are his best films. After his expatriation from Russia, there is an undeniable decline in quality, partially due to the frustrating conditions of utility, as noted by Susan Sontag in an unrelated *New York Times* piece on cinema: '... The

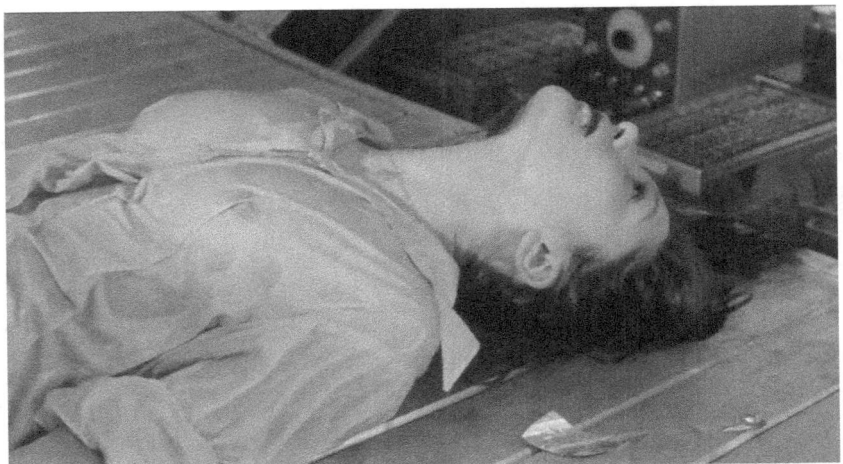

Comparative stills from Solaris *and* Stalker. © *Mosfilm*

internationalizing of financing and therefore of casts were disastrous for Andrei Tarkovsky in the last two films of his stupendous (and tragically abbreviated) career.' But financed or not, Tarkovsky's depictions of women in the otherwise brilliant *Nostalghia* leave the viewer aghast. In his essay 'Tarkovsky's *Nostalghia*: Beauty in maddeningly antifeminist visual poetry', Anthony V. LeClair agonizes over Tarkovsky's weak female leads in the film:

> Just as with [*The Mirror, Stalker,* and *Solaris*] there is an economy of dialogue within *Nostalghia*. And in many ways the long bouts of silence between meaty scenes of dialogue is for the best, for, when Tarkovsky speaks through his characters, he lets loose a barrage of staunchly anti-feminist ideals. Here, Tarkovsky vehemently and actively idealizes and idolizes the figure of motherhood while calling out women who are searching, instead, for happiness. And though, certainly, the two are not mutually exclusive, Tarkovsky paints them as dichotomous—one, virtuous and holy, the other, selfish and naïve. [...] To Tarkovsky, motherhood is an incredible ascetic virtue, and the all giving, sacrificial role of the mother country and the motherly figure are worshipped throughout the film. Visually, they are some of the most beautiful pictures put to camera. A pregnant woman in black laying in repose, an abundance of birds emerging from the womb of a maternal effigy, generations of women and children standing among the hills of a picturesque Russian countryside. Devoid of context, they are awe-inspiring.

It is a little shocking, a little incredulous to us today, to think that an intellectual auteur as far-reaching as Tarkovsky, who succeeds so monumentally with groundbreaking philosophical themes in his films, tackling human dignity and spirituality with such an expert vision and skill, could be so utterly inadept at understanding the internality of femininity. A slight reprieve for *Stalker*, is that its sexism pales in comparison to that aforementioned in *Nostalghia*. Stalker's Wife is more absent than she is offensive in a sexist portrayal and so, while *Stalker* is certainly not passing the Bechdel Test any time soon, it's not so much offensive in content, as it is void of female input.

Porcupine

Porcupine, aside from the three main characters, is probably the 'mentioned' character most worthy of examination. As briefly noted earlier, he is endlessly intriguing. Though he does not actually appear in the film, he is referred to again and again. Porcupine was Stalker's mentor, a stalker himself, devastated by the loss of his brother within the Zone as he was killed by the Meat Grinder. When Porcupine reaches the Room—although stalkers are not supposed to ever enter the Room themselves—he does so anyway, hoping his deepest desire, the resurrection of his brother, will occur. It does not. Instead, when he returns home, he finds himself immensely wealthy, whereupon he promptly hangs himself. There are many interesting theories as to the increased mentions of Porcupine throughout the film. A popular internet fan theory is that Porcupine might be Stalker's father. Another, that Stalker might actually be Porcupine's brother himself, and he did not actually die—which is why the Room would refuse Porcupine's desire of a resurrection that cannot possibly be: it can't revive a person who is already living, and instead, gave him his second greatest desire. Porcupine, insofar as he operates as both a character in the story as well as potentially, an alternative illusionary narrative device, is rather effective.[6]

Little Monkey

Little Monkey is barely in the film at all but cannot be understated in her importance. She is Stalker's handicapped daughter, but also possesses an implied special Otherness and therein the ability of telekinesis: in the film's end sequence, she sits at a table and appears to drag a glass across it with her mind.[7] In addition to her character, Monkey also operates as a plot synecdoche for the Room itself. Her Otherness is cryptic and unspecified, only hinted at in the fleeting final moments of the film. She is damaged, crippled, much like the dystopic uninhabited landscape of the Zone has been ravaged by nature as well, unfairly and prematurely laid to waste, by no fault of her own. We don't know exactly how/if Monkey received her powers. We assume her powers come from the Zone, the Room specifically, and that Stalker somehow is responsible for her ailments, which sets the scene for the film's narrative most plausibly. Monkey doesn't speak during the film, except for the voiceover of the poem in the conclusion. Her character elicits all the anticipatable traumatic visages of a child growing up in her circumstances, invoking sympathy easily from us, but moreover a curiosity regarding her inconclusive origins and relation to the grander continuing mystery of the Zone itself, the indeterminable space.

Endnotes

6. I say 'alternative' because unlike a more clichéd or lazy 'out' of a situation, which is a more typically generic usage of the device, Porcupine *is* used as the link to explain away several eyebrow-raising moments of the plot—i.e. Stalker's being able to explain away effects of the Room, why a stalker should not enter the room, the caustic literality of the Room's Otherness. In contrast to a more typical Deus Ex Machina, which might offer an easy solution for the cryptic uncertainties of the Zone.
7. It has been argued that potentially the explanation for her telekinesis is simply that the nearby trains that so often shake everything in Stalker's apartment (as indeed, can be heard during this scene and the opening scene) are the cause of the shaking glass moving across the table. This explanation should and will be compiled within larger theories regarding the Room as being entirely ordinate.

Inside the Zone

'Here we are...standing on the doorstep. It's the most important moment...in your life. You must know that...your most cherished desire will come true here. Your sincerest wish, the desire that has made you suffer most. There's no need to speak. You must only...concentrate and recall all of your past life. When a man thinks of the past, he becomes kinder. But the main thing ...The main thing...you must believe. Ok, now you can go. Who wants to go first? Perhaps you?' – Stalker (*Stalker*, 1979)

© *Daisy Braun*

Tarkovsky's *Stalker* is a science-fiction film split in two parts. The first half largely depicts the world outside the Zone and the trio's path to get inside. The latter half, the journey through the interior to its heart, the Room. The Zone is a gorgonizing labyrinth, frustrating and cryptic to analyze, amplified by Tarkovsky's irritating insistence that the Zone was a simple landscape and should be utterly disregarded in terms of critical analysis regarding its symbolism or device. Obviously, this is not the case and the varying meanings of the space is incredibly intriguing. To understand the Zone we have to examine it as four parts. First, the geographical Zone to be taken quite literally; the space itself. Second, Then, the Zone as it operates with regards to its fantasmatic elements.[8] The Zone as a symbolic manifestation, and lastly, the Zone as it pertains to its illocutionary function: what the Zone means to those who travel in it. *Stalker* begins with what we can surmise as an archived interview, an explanation of the Zone from one Professor Wallace, a recipient of the Nobel Prize, interviewed by a journalist for RAI (Radiotelevisione Italia). Even if you're going into this film completely blind, it becomes quickly apparent that the Zone will be the place of interest for the narrative. The Zone we receive visually is not even the original landscape envisioned by Tarkovsky for the film, since the reshoots took them to Estonia. Setting for Tarkovsky is essential. And though he himself might have dismissed it, the Unknowable and fantastical quality of the Zone is essential as well. We cannot abide by his wishes here—to examine *Stalker* without a thorough observation of the Zone would be absurd, pointless. And yes, perhaps the Room—and by extension the Zone— is ambiguous in nature, but it is utterly important to attempt to explicitly and implicitly understand why it is open-ended and what its possibilities might mean.

The space of the Zone in and of itself is unnerving: a disturbed personification of the Anthropocene.[9] Looking at the Zone from an ecological perspective, it is difficult to argue against this. Jesse Montgomery in his essay 'What is the Zone and Are We in It?' borrows from Susan Sontag, when he describes the Anthropocene and its register in *Stalker* as traversing through once natural landscapes that have been silently terrorized by some ineffable or possibility thermonuclear force, the 'unremitting banality of inconceivable terror', and the film's plot 'anticipates a future that is slow and incomprehensible ... where we unwittingly cross crucial thresholds like sleepwalkers as we search for something that finally appears, in the wrong room' (26). The Zone is more frequently posed as an ineffable science-fiction allegory, likely for its comparative ease of explanation, compared to the more convoluted theory of the Zone operating or resulting from the consequential affect of anthropological manifest on landscape, and subsequent regrowth or overgrowth of nature in the absence of the invasive humanity. The Zone as a landscape is sparse—it is green but overgrown and unkempt, it is beautiful, but ravaged by disaster, environmental or otherwise; the mind trends towards nuclear disaster first because of the resemblance to Chernobyl and the shots later in the film of Stalker and his family on the small beach beneath a giant nuclear facility. There is a lingering sense of the traumas of the Second World War as well; throughout the journey, Stalker tests the pathways by throwing strips of cloth tied to metal nuts to set off any potentially armed traps, landmines, etc. Nothing ever comes of this, which might lead to furthering one's suspicion that there *aren't* any traps, but either way, it's unsettling. More than anything else, it is the *lack of humanity* that is responsible for the overgrowth of botanic beauty and unsettling quality of the Zone. While we must acknowledge the Zone at its innermost as separated from the outside world in its presence, as a psychic space, the visceral quality of its landscape is just so eerie. It sets a strong precedent of film setting; the unnerving element of a place that, once inhabited by many people, no longer is.

Entire film franchises have seen been predicated on that very notion, ranging from Danny Boyle's *28 Days Later* (2002) to *The Survivalist* (2016). The absence of humanity is so startling to us, yet beneath this, there's always humanity lurking around the corner, from the skeletal remains of a couple, to the telephone, and so on. The Zone returns to 'the now' a present that is not even past. Consider the Zone as a possibly-extraterrestrial thing, an indeterminable Other, capable of fantasmatic acts; but also, an entirely natural thing. The overgrowth of nature in the Zone is evident, mostly emphasized in its absence of humanity, but even without that focus, you can see easily that there is *nature* everywhere. When we enter the Zone we see abandoned Soviet tanks and platoon-troop carriers covered in moss, we even get a shot of the three travelers moving forward from inside one of the carriers, encased in the leaves and moss, giving a nice panoramic image of the Anthropocene, the men crossing the threshold of human influx on nature.

Consider some famous films similar in tone, atmosphere, or philosophy with *Stalker*. Films like 砂の女/*Woman in the Dunes* (1964), *Jeanne Dielman 23 Quai du Commerce 1080 Bruxelles* (1975), and *Upstream Color* (2013). Directors Teshigahara, Akerman and Carruth all created films that surpass any expectation of simple entertainment, bringing in a range of impressive filmmaking, ranging in specificity from thoughtful, to stressed, to tearfully frustrating. These cultured responses are intentional and are access points for defining how *mise-en-scène* ought to be conveyed in cinema. Would *Jeanne Dielman*'s dread-inducing ennui of total lifeless claustrophobia be at all captivating if it was not so carefully and accurately constructed? Unlikely. As much as Tarkovsky seemed keen on avoiding these critical dissections of the Zone, they were inevitable. Its fantasmatic elements are eye-catchy, in the same way we are drawn to the magical elements of absurd surrealism in fiction, like a Franz Kafka novel. Vincenzo Natali's surreal film *Cube* (1997) owes a lot to *Stalker* as it plays primarily into the essentiality of its Kafkaesque space, utilizing the space as central for the plot; almost the entirety of the film was shot in one square room. The film features a group of unrelated people who awaken inside the gigantic cube, comprised of rooms on each side, each room connecting to six other rooms. It's enormous and moves on its own, autonomously, changing up the combinations of which room connects to which. While the cube of *Cube* certainly does not wield the same mysticism of *Stalker*'s Zone, when you consider its vast size and outer-shell, it does cast itself as implausible as existing without some element of science-fiction involved in its creation. So, do these characters discover how or why they landed in this cube? Or indeed, what purpose the cube serves? No. But like the Zone, it hardly matters.

The deliberately ambiguous aspects of the Zone are always cast out as such, leading it to be used with emphasis on the intentionality of uncertainty. In the current film scope, we might call it Lynchian, that axiom of achieving atmospheric perfection before a consideration to linear narrative, and indeed, it is difficult to imagine the achievements of a film like *Mullholland Drive* (2001) without roadwork paved by *Stalker*.[10] The unknown is especially exciting when it's put into conversation with science-fiction films, since it's a direct-line in that wheelhouse. We are subsequently denied any essential anthropological information we might find comforting, and instead, the information we *don't have* leads the story, consequential or not. Think of the graphic novel *Y: The Last Man* where the world's entire population of mammals with Y chromosomes (all human males) all simultaneously die in an instant, except the protagonist and his pet capuchin monkey. They spend the entirety of the comic's six-year run searching for an answer, a reason for the mass-extinction, and in doing so, dozens of theories are provided and explored—but the answer is never actually given. It becomes entirely unimportant, because like Tarkovsky, its author Brian K. Vaughan viewed the origin of the phenomena as a landscaping tool for the development of his characters and their world. So while the drive for information does lead the plot, the answer is entirely irrelevant to it. This must be done carefully, like needlework; so many films unravel with an unexplainable element that simply irritates, that does not work, and leaves audiences with an unsavory feeling towards what is, undoubtedly, weak art. Leaving an unknowable entity that can do whatever it wants, because of unknowability is lazy and moviegoers (even contemptible ones) notice these things and dismiss them. Rian Johnson's sci-fi thriller *Looper* (2012) is an example; in some ways it's an exciting film, it's not half-bad. But the film revolves around a time travel mechanism that is gossamer thin, which not only takes you out of the film when you must involuntarily pause to think about it (to deconstruct it and rendering it failed), but equally you also wind up with a plot that feels irritatingly familiar, thin, and equally implausible. So even if all the other elements of cinema are working, the film falls apart.

Returning for a moment to the Strugatsky brothers, the title of their novel *Roadside Picnic* is a helpful indicator—it refers directly to the aliens/visitors who originally created the mysterious zone (though in the original novel there were six.) Their stay on the planet was brief; they found Earth uninteresting and so they left. The mythos of the Zone itself, while grand in scale to the stalkers and their parties, is actually relatively dull to the aliens themselves, analogous to human decay or rubble left behind after a picnic one might have on a road-trip. Recall the Duchampian antique pot anecdote told by the Writer when we first meet him:

> Say there's some antique pot in a museum. In its own time, it was a trash bin. But now it draws admiration for its simplicity of line and unique form. And everyone 'oohs' and 'aahs' over it. Suddenly, it turns out not to be an antique at all. It was planted by some joker for a laugh, in order to make some fun. The sounds of admiration die away. Some connoisseurs!

The mundanity of the object, counteracts its meaninglessness with artificial mysticism, giving it a disembodied but sublime quality. It's not uncommon to see in any given narrative—in *Raiders of the Lost Ark* (1981) when Indiana Jones confronts his adversary, the French archeologist Belloq at a hookah bar in Cairo, Belloq holds up a brass pocket-watch: 'Look at this ... it's worthless ... ten dollars from a vendor in the street. But, I take it, I bury it in the sand for a thousand years, it becomes priceless ... like the Ark. Men will kill for it. Men like you and me.' Belloq is on the money: in *Stalker,* like *Raiders*, these men pay unknown but balefully vast fees to even attempt to voyage into the Zone with Stalker though it is known they may be maimed or die. The belief in the Room is strong enough, or, moreover, desirable enough to make the odds of success a non-contention And of course, in the end, Stalker's two companions both refuse to enter the Room. Which given the immense toll they have racked up so far, financially, mentally and emotionally, the question as to whether the Room is even real at all, becomes more persistent and urgent. At the finale of *Raiders of the Lost Ark*, Indiana Jones and Marion Ravenwood avert their eyes from the opened Lost Ark, which promptly kills everyone who was looking at its unveiling—they don't see, but it doesn't matter, the message is clear.

Solaris

The best or most coherent way to comprehend the journey into the belly of ineffable elements presented in the Zone and, notably, the Room of *Stalker* is to put it into conversation with Tarkovsky's other great science-fiction film, *Solaris*. The primary distinction between the two, hinges on self-sacrifice and articulation. Solaris grants your desires; The Room does not. Both Solaris and the Room bring Nietzsche to the forefront of the mind; perspectivism leads us to a cruel reality where there are no absolute truths to be had; be they generated truths or the inability to generate truths. But the contrasts of the two fantasmatic desire machines are most intriguing. Consider this analysis by Lacanian philosopher and psychoanalyst Slavoj Žižek:

> ...In *Solaris*, we get id-machines, an object which realizes your nightmares, desires, fears, even before you ask for it, as it were. In *Stalker* it's the opposite, a zone where your desires, deepest wishes get realized on condition that you are able to formulate them. Which, of course, you are never able, which is why everybody

fails once you get there in the center of the zone. Solution to this tension is that of religious obscurantism. [...] Tarkovskian subjects, when they pray, they don't look up, they look down. They even sometimes, as in *Stalker*, put their head directly onto the earth. Here, I think Tarkovsky affects us at a level which is much deeper, much more crucial for our experience than all the standard, spiritual motives of elevating ourselves above material reality and so on. There is nothing specific about the zone. It's purely a place where a certain limit is set. You set a limit, you put a certain zone off-limit and although things remain exactly the way they were, it's perceived as another place. Precisely as the place onto which you can project your beliefs, your fears, things from your inner space. In other words, the zone is ultimately the very whiteness of the cinematic screen (223-224).

Žižek (rather characteristically) categorizes the Zone as a Lacanian tool of fantasmatic Otherness, a reading of an 'indeterminate space'. *Solaris*—Tarkovsky's version— concludes itself with a cruel false image: the manufactured false reunion of father and son, a materialized simulacrum created by the planet to satiate the protagonist Kelvin from leaving it. Planet Solaris—while it is a Thing that cannot itself be understood fully, can resemble somewhat that indeterminable libidinal energy, attractive and inexorable; abstractly, it's almost blinding in its attractiveness to us, whereas the Zone, while it is known to contain ineffable energy as well, keeps it in a contained, obtainable space. If you can make it to the Room, it is thought you can obtain the desires: your innermost desires. Then, the actuality of both the Solaris-Thing and the Zone are contortions of the same origin-thoughts: for Solaris, not their actual mesmeric desires, but a twisted, traumatic realized fantasy. For the Room, it's not necessarily twisted, but it is in fact, unreachable. If you can enter the Room you will not be capable of realizing that innermost desire anyway, so it is ineffably unobtainable. A gritty post-Lacanian thought: perhaps realized fantasy completely ruins any enjoyment. Kelvin reuniting with his dead-wife Hari, now resurrected in *Solaris* is nothing sure of *pure* terror, a nightmare, more phantasmagoria than any kind of reality, and yet, *very* real. It is not in the slightest bit fantastical once it is realized. *Stalker*, however, gives us instead the faith-based problem: unlike *Solaris* our protagonists know going into the Zone what the fantasmatic element pertains, so there is a level of hesitancy regarding what is unknown: they don't really *know*

Kelvin and Hari from Solaris. © *Mosfilm*

what they truly desire, so what will they achieve? This is addressed in a recount from Stalker regarding his mentor, Porcupine, who became emotionally destroyed by this own misconception of his own personal desires.

The planet, Solaris, with its generative consciousness is—pleasantly—and ostensibly void of the faith-dilemma of the Room. When Kelvin awakens each time Hari is resurrected, her sentience has grown, regardless of his acceptance/rejection of her existence being valid or not. She and Solaris both exist and manifest their fantasmatic qualities regardless of the desires, fears and agonies of the cosmonauts it preys upon. Kelvin, at first, couldn't be further from Stalker; he arrives at the Solaris space station very cynical about the whole experience, seemingly keen on the prospect of concluding the studies of the planet, not really believing the stories from Berton, of unusual and fantastical experiences generated from the planet. Like Stalker, he becomes enveloped in the Otherness, unavoidably falling for the artificial-Hari. Such becomes his devotion to the projections of the planet, that he chooses to remain there, collapsing at the feet of the artificialized version of his father on the Solaris Island. And, as Žižek notes, once you begin to try and actualize the fantasies curated for you by the Solaris-Other, that generates its projections from the id-based desires of the cosmonauts, once you attempt to live out that fantasy, it of course, becomes nightmare (228). The primary difference with the Room comes from its inability to grant the wish, regardless of its desirability. That said, the meaning of the Room, e.g. implicatively, still resonates with a partially transcendental condition, wherein the Room itself is constructible to us in a liminal sense, but as an abstraction is not a full-blown concept to the extent that it could explain the preconditions of its transcendental resonance the way narratively Solaris does. This works well for the concept of faith in Stalker and the faith of the Stalker himself. If he believes in the power of the Room, then when he brings people to it, if they are able to walk into it and conceive their innermost desire, and then it comes true, he can affirm his beliefs and continue the pilgrimages. We ought to consider the Room *without* the faith-based question, as well. If the determinacy of the Room to grant the deepest desire of its entrant hinged only on True Faith alone, how then could its discovery been made originally? If one were to argue that it must have had an initial experience to the first entrant, unaware of the Room's abilities, then perhaps the Room can change or alter itself, conditionally. In some regard, we begin to view the Room more like the planet Solaris, a sentient Other, we move closer to a viable Room that does possess a fantasmatic element. Can Stalker still have a religious fixation and faith-based dilemma if this is the case? Yes, of course.

The strongest evidence for the existence of the Room comes in the form of Monkey, Stalker's daughter. The infamous final short of the film—Monkey sitting solemnly at the table staring at several glasses of liquid that then slide on their own, autonomously across it—cannot be understated in its significance to the plot as a whole, or regarding the argument for the Room's viability. If we take Monkey at face value, if we see her as telekinetic, then, it's difficult to argue that the Room isn't fantastical—how else could she have come by these abilities? The fact that she is *both* handicapped and possessing of psychic abilities not only proves this, but can also be read as implicative—potentially, Stalker or his wife entered the Room with the girl to cure her, and instead, the Room gave her these abilities. It is the kind of misdirected blessing that the Room would sequester. It can also be argued though, that this is all entirely misdirection; the last scene can be explained away rationally as well, with the local trains passing by, with enough ferocity to shake the glasses that Monkey is staring at across the table. We do in fact see the shaking caused by these trains in the apartment during the opening of the film. This would support the so-framed 'ordinate' reading of the film, but clearly it is left open-ended to be interpreted either way.

The Meat Grinder

Aside from the Room itself, the most fascinating aspect of the Zone is the Meat Grinder, which begins with a pipe that leads the trio through the sandy dunes into the penultimate room-before-the-Room, with the telephone. The Meat Grinder is the most treacherous location in the Zone, Stalker informs us of this, after they reunite with Writer who enters the penultimate room first: 'You must have been through such agony. This pipe is the most terrible part of the Zone, we call it "meat grinder", how many people has it ground up? It is worse than any meat grinder. So many people have perished here. And it was there Porcupine laid his brother.' One of the most highly contentious aspects of the film, is the sound of the Meat Grinder sequence. Originally, Eduard Artemyev, the film's composer had scored a delicate, sparse piece, specifically for that sequence which Tarkovsky had admired but felt unsure of. Artemyev, insisted in an interview conducted in 2000, released by Criterion Collection that the journey through the tunnel of the Grinder would have been better illustrated with his piece:

> I also remember making a record in Holland. [...] I included it in a melody written for *Stalker*, it was called 'A Long Walk', for the scene when the heroes walk down the pipe, that passage. I wrote the music—Tarkovsky said it was good. When I came to the recording, I saw Tarkovsky was putting it on and off. I asked him what the matter was; he said that if he could do without music, he wouldn't use it at all. He just didn't need any music there. It was a rhythmic melody...it put you in a state of meditation. But, he needed no music there. I began to watch him very closely. I came to each recording session. Then Tarkovsky decided that he couldn't do without music. I relaxed and stopped coming...and he took it off! At the last moment he eliminated it from the film. I believe his wish to hold out without music was wrong. I watched that film many times, and the music is missing there.

> Maybe not this kind of music, maybe some other music...

It's hard to agree with Artemyev (albeit difficult to disagree without the track as evidence) but the stilly-silence of Writer's terrified solitary trek through the grinder while Professor and Stalker wait anxiously watching is breathtaking, the only sound being slight running water and his feet on the murky wetness of the pipe. It's hard to imagine any music, regardless of its transcendental or haunting quality might be accurate to capture the absolute underground-silence of the tunnel, it's a very specific nonsound. In general though, the music of the Zone is ethereal, meditative, and trance-like. Somewhat comparative to the Meat Grinder sequence—regards its intensity—comes earlier in the film, when Writer, irritated by Stalker's cautious pathway to the Room, which will take them much longer, insists on walking the straightest, fastest path towards the building leading to the Room. Cynical though he is regarding the other-worldly fantasmatic elements of the Zone, he seems unnerved as he approaches the structure and then, suddenly, we hear an indecipherable voice tell him to go back. The film is intentionally ambiguous on the origin of the voice, but options are that it is (a) a disembodied voice created by the Zone itself; (b) Stalker disguising his voice telling Writer to retreat; (c) Writer himself pretending to tell himself this, as he is too frightened to continue on his own.

Innermost Zones

The world of *Stalker* operates in a place that resides after an unknown amount of time following the initiating incident—birthing of the Zone. Since then, there's a developed mythos around the parameters, the powers of the Zone, who made it, why, and so on. Half the fun of the thing is acknowledging an impossibility in deciphering exactly what is true and what is not. Jonathan Nolan's been given a tremendous amount of praise for his revitalization of *Westworld* (2017–), an HBO revision of the 70s sci-fi western film based on the novel by Michael Crichton. *Westworld* has acknowledged its enormous Tarkovskian inspiration for the show—a second season episode was even considered an homage to *Stalker* according to a *Variety* interview with director Lisa Joy. Tarkovsky is very present in its cinematography and sound. What seems to resonate with audiences of the program is the synchronicity of the Real and the Simulation. But what's far more interesting in the construct of the narrative is the point which is reached by the end of the first series of *Westworld*, the what-if-perhaps-it's-all-real moment, where the androids begin to experience a true consciousness. This is a far larger topic than can be permitted here, obviously, so let's focus on Westworld itself, this defined fantasy space where wealthy men can act out their absurd sexualized hero fantasies for a hefty cost. Like the forgettable recent Spielberg film *Ready Player One* (2018) the lamentable love of the virtual, of nostalgia, is dull and dismissible. But, unlike that film, there is something here, with *Westworld*. Like the idiosyncratic journey Stalker takes his companions on through the Zone, Westworld has distinct rules and determinations that dictate its narrative. The impatient Professor forgoes Stalker's instructions during the journey in the Zone, akin to some of the Westworld guests who try to facilitate their own ends through the place—create their own pathways to achieve whatever ends, often with uniquely tragic results. If you know science-fiction narrative you know the story doesn't end well for humans playing god with robots. Similarly, things don't go well for the Stalker trio when they finally reach the Room. Upon standing at its precipice, Stalker says to the other two:

> Here we are...standing on the doorstep. It's the most important moment...in your life. You must know that...your most cherished desire will come true here. Your sincerest wish, the desire that has made you suffer most. There's no need to speak. You must only...concentrate and recall all of your past life. When a man thinks of the past, he becomes kinder. But the main thing – ...The main thing...you must believe. Ok, now you can go. Who wants to go first? Perhaps you?

In the Zone, you are your innermost self, the you from which the Room will generate your truest desire. According to Robert Bird, the Zone's limit itself: 'is the primary condition for the "presence of the other", the source of "the voice that sustains desire". In many respects the Zone is simply the demarcated area within which an event can occur' (68-69). The Zone is as Bird says, a place void of personhood, the vacancy is central to the unraveling of the ego leaving its incumbents as uncertain, or as Žižek puts it, an 'indeterminacy of what lies beyond the limit' (229). Not only in its function as ineffable space, but also in time—and indeed the passage of time in the place seems very surreal and unclear. Philosopher Gilles Deleuze agrees, in *Cinema 2:*

The Time-Image where he writes:

> [Tarkovsky] says that what is essential is the way time flows in the show, its tension or rarefaction, 'the pressure of time in the shot'. [...] It is only when the sign opens directly onto time, when time provides the signaletic material itself, that the type, which has become temporal, coincides with the feature of singularity separated from its motor associations. It is here that Tarkovsky's wish comes true: that 'the cinematographer succeeds in fixing time in its indices [in its signs] perceptible by the senses'. And, in a sense, cinema had always done this; but, in another sense, it could only realize that it had in the course of its evolution, thanks to a crisis of the movement-image (42-43).

Deleuze, when he speaks of the indices[11] disbursed by Tarkovsky throughout the film, is speaking of his films as successfully immersing their audiences in the immanence of narrative, in the time of the film. Tarkovsky succeeds with that *pressure of time* as utilized in the Zone—it becomes more than a measurement of distance or narrative. The lethargy of the journey is useful in the process of deconstructing a more conventional film-time depiction; when the trio stops to rest frequently, when they move around easier pathways and slowly tie the cloths to the metal nuts.

Stalker himself, is aware of these unnatural feature elements of the Zone. Pointedly, in their journey he cautions his companions to try and embody the past: 'When a man is born, he is weak and supple, when he dies—he is strong and callous... suppleness and weakness express the freshness of living. That is why what has hardened will not win.' And then again as quoted on the verge of the Room: '... Concentrate and recall all of your past life. When a person thinks of his past he becomes kinder.' Outside the world of the Zone, this is a peculiar claim. From what we understand psychoanalytically regarding inherited traumas and the intergenerational nature of grief, it's not difficult to object to, or at least find difficulty with this claim—Writer clearly agrees with this dissuasion as he remarks coldly that remembering his past will hardly make him kinder. Regardless, the Room will certainly work better for you, if you're certain...

...If that is, the Room works at all, which again, remains unknown. Tarkovsky consistently dismissed the Zone and the Room again and again, leading viewers to question the Zone as just a big swindle. Tarkovsky is on the record giving contradictory explanations: 'The Zone doesn't exist. Stalker himself invented the Zone. He created it, so that he would be able to bring there some unhappy persons and impose on them the idea of hope. The room of desires is equally Stalker's creation, yet another provocation in the face of the material world' (Cosse, 169). But he also said, in a separate interview, '...In the Strugatsky story, the desires were truly fulfilled, whereas in the script this remains a mystery. You don't know whether this is true or whether it's the Stalker's fantasy. For me as the author of the film, either choice is OK' (Tassone, 55). It's not so clear if we can take either of these claims at face value though, or if it's Tarkovsky toying with media journalists, who he does not respect. Because of all the substance built up around the Zone—the military barricade and known existence of the Zone by the common populous—we can at least assume that if the Zone is fictive, then it is a fiction unknown to an entire generation or even generations of believers, including Stalker himself, whose daughter may or may not have been crippled and gifted with telekinetic abilities by the Zone. Tarkovsky certainly enjoyed being adversarial in his interviews and he shouldn't be taken without a grain of salt when speaking about the Zone and the Room.

Unlike the virtual unreality of simulated worlds like Westworld, it is clear that what happens in the Zone is very real. The three travelers speak often of Porcupine and his brother, both of whom are now dead due to their experiences in the Room. Kierkegaard writes often of an existential sphere or space, one that can be sequenced by a higher power, an ends-justify-the-means by reason of faith-based absolution. This, is why Stalker's Wife—though in despair—ultimately supports his unfaltering intention to continue guiding clients into the Zone. And indeed, there is a lush source of religious symbolism to support Stalker's faith in it, in every moment in the Zone. Perhaps faith for Kierkegaard is as it is for Stalker too: think about Victor Fleming's *The Wizard of Oz* (1939) where the existence of Oz is irrelevant but the belief in his actuality, the faith element is what transforms the lives of the heroes. Such is likely the same for Stalker; regardless of the truth of the Zone, Stalker's life is irreducibly linked to it. For Tarkovsky the dilemma of the Zone comes in its '...death of spirituality as a result of our possessing false knowledge' (159). Tarkovsky's last films (certainly *Stalker* and *The Sacrifice*) hinge on the idea of necessitating one's personal faith in the pursuit for meaning and human dignity. Like Kierkegaard, Tarkovsky has no time for constructs of dispassionate objectivity in truth, rather forged through leaps of faith and choice. Which makes the silence of the presence of the Room's fantasmatic element in the film all the more fascinating.

Sometimes, it's more entertaining as a viewer to just settle the fantasmatic element in one's mind; when it benefits the film it can be enticing to do this. A strong example of this critical distance from the element comes from Yorgos Lanthimos in his film *The Killing of a Sacred Deer* (2017). There's an unknowable curse-like virus that begins slowly killing the family of a cardiothoracic surgeon named Steven Murphy. We never learn the true conditions or origin of the ailment plaguing the three—son, daughter, and wife. We are only ever able to have the ailment partially explained from an unreliable narrator, in the form of the film's antagonist, the psychotic Martin, who claims to be causing the unknowable illness as a retribution for the death of his father—who Murphy killed while intoxicated, performing surgery some six months previous. Akin to his previous films, *The Lobster* (2016) and *Κυνόδοντα/Dogtooth* (2009), Lanthimos establishes an unknowable condition in his film, often absurd or irrelevant to the actual plot of the film. A bad-tempered audience might balk at the frustration of not having all their questions answered by film's end, but it's entirely irrelevant to what he is doing with his plot. Of course, we want to know, but we can't. Just like Tarkovsky's film; understanding the exact conditions of the Zone comes from our most diligent desire to obsessively relate with the film, to identify it fully—this seems to come more and more from a film culture intimately familiar with the process of world-building, which is admirable in its enthusiasms, but entirely unimportant in enjoying a film. *The Killing of a Sacred Deer* doesn't need you to understand why things are happening, it needs you to accept that they are and that they will. Once you do this, you are able to appreciate the incredulous helplessness of its protagonists in their circumstance, and then the daunting camerawork, the threatening soundtrack and atmosphere of the Murphy's house can take hold. It's a more traditional and concrete *mise-en-scène* that is completely accessible once you accept the conditions of its outline, within the world of *The Killing of Sacred Deer*'s gaze, and its outset limitations.

Understanding the Zone may have been made slightly easier, with a recent film that includes an antithesis of it. Lars Von Trier's film *Antichrist* (2009) takes place predominately in an eerie and cerebral forest setting called Eden. A controversial film, minimal like *Stalker*, the film is in fact, dedicated to Tarkovsky. The visual and thematic allusions to *Stalker* in it—and of Tarkovsky films in general—are far too numerous to mention, but refreshingly to say, it is conducted in a satisfactory original way, as opposed to a reductive derivative quality. The film can be quite unpleasant and disgusting in its treatment of women, but the film is equal in the ever-present plot, always dwelling within the slightest boundaries of the fantasmatic elements. Author Geoff Dyer, (though he perhaps blunders in dismissing *Antichrist* as irritatingly diminutive in relation to *Stalker*), does expertly credit Eden as the successful anti-Zone in his book *Zona*. The Zone grants your deepest inner desires, whereas Eden acts as a monster-Solaris Island, where your darkest nightmares come to pass. Certainly, *Antichrist* is no *Stalker*, though an admirable additional tribute text to Tarkovsky. When in conversation with the Zone it's an intriguing addition because they aren't mirror opposites—they're both often gruesome and grueling to endure; the anti-Zone is not black-and-white in its operative conditions either, like the Zone itself, because of its unique quality of difference—it's a worthy aside to take, it's esoteric but helpful. The virtue of suffering through Eden, though clandestine, becomes clear; it's a season in hell surely, but a season nonetheless. The same is true with the Zone.

If we treat the Room as less of a Cave Allegory—a meek interpretation[12]—and more of a Biblical Eden—to differentiate from the just-mentioned Von Trier Eden—we can understand where a lot of Stalker's anxiety might come from; the dread he exhibits for most of the journey through the Zone, and much of the time after departing from it as well. Eden—according to Kierkegaard, at least—has Adam, before the concept of Good and Evil, experiencing the anxiety of the Apple. Similarly, Stalker—or stalkers in general as practitioners of the Zone—suffer and agonize over the supposed consequences of a stalker entering the Room, which is strictly forbidden.

It is impossible to ignore the political implications of the Zone as well: a guarded military site, disallowing civilians to any access. Visually, as Dyer remarks in his conversation with the Criterion Collection's release of *Stalker*: 'You can't watch *Stalker* and not think about the gulags. It's not about the Gulag but it's *there*.' And Žižek as well: 'For a citizen of the defunct Soviet Union, the notion of a forbidden Zone is

(1) Gulag ... (2) a territory poisoned or otherwise rendered uninhabitable by some technological (biochemical, nuclear...) catastrophe like Chernobyl' (225). The Zone is unnerving in that it does transcend its very medium into the actual world in this way—it is often said the Chernobyl Disaster, which took place seven years after the film's Soviet release has an unexplainable visual similarity to the film. The area was even supposedly referred to as 'the Zone of alienation' and those who were tasked with caring for the abandoned nuclear power plant are supposed to have referred to themselves as 'stalkers', in reference to the film. But remembering again, this was nearly a decade later, a strange coincidence. Specifically, Tarkovsky was predicting more than Chernobyl with his film, as John A. Riley notes in his essay on the film, it was: 'the ongoing relevance of the border, the zone, and our uneasy relation to our collective past' (20). Riley is correct—the Zone, inasmuch as it resides behind walls, behind AK-47s, is more about the cultural pilgrimage than the Otherness of the thing itself. The Zone has been sought after to be used over and over, presumably by both those who have entered the room, like Porcupine and the other stalkers, who operate as profiteers around it. If we do view the Zone as the Strugatsky Brothers' originally conceived it, as a roadside picnic of no existential significance, then this obsessive behavior by governmental and military forces, by profiteers and its spiritual hopefuls, *is* an illocutionary way of relating to both the past, and for those who seek entrance into the Zone, a success of faith.

There is a common recurrent in postwar science-fiction films: the ineffable or fantasmatic element of the film, typically also the acting fear object, is a stand-in for the looming threat of nuclear holocaust. This is certainly not the only time in history that culture has permeated art in this way, but it occurs with enough frequency to be noticed here. *Stalker* is difficult to pin down as a nuclear allegory, but just like the augmented presence of the shadows of the gulags, there is, at the very least, the strong specter of nuclear fear present at all times in and out of the Zone. The natural growth of the Zone—it is quite a green place, especially in contrast to the sickly outside world—is intriguing if we examine the sickish appearance of Stalker—physically he looks like someone who has encountered far too much radiation, which registers as acceptable to us as an audience, since he is constantly sneaking into the Zone. But then, *is* it radioactive? It is most often claimed by film theorists that the

Stalker and family, beneath a nuclear powerplant. © Mosfilm

Zone itself is a visual representation by Tarkovsky directly inspired by, or even based on the 1957 Kyshtym nuclear disaster, a large radioactive contamination that occurred at a plutonium site in Ozyorsk, Chelyabinsk Oblast. The Chelyabinsk area is one of the most heavily polluted in the world, and the areas of the EURT (East Urals Radioactive Trace) are still dangerously radioactive to this day, more than 60 years later.

It's unclear how literally we are supposed to take the radiation of the Zone. If we, like Stalker, take everything on faith, we believe it to be a place of extraterrestrial origins. If so, is it still likely radioactive? Yes, probably. What about the alternative? The Zone simply being the result of a nuclear Kyshtym-esque situation gone awry certainly would explain the high levels of military presence around it and general public intrigue at the mystery surrounding its existence. Tarkovsky scholars tend to make reference more commonly to Chernobyl—likely because of its notability—than to Kyshtym, but Chernobyl also seems to better echo the inhabitability of the Zone, as Chernobyl's Exclusion Zone is still uninhabitable.[13] If the Zone is radioactive what does that mean for the stalkers and their clientele? It would depend on how bad the radiation levels were, which gets complex fast. But we can gather based on Monkey, who was born disabled, and Stalker's physical signs of debilitation, that it is at least, unhealthy to be there.

The notion of transfusing nuclear disaster or impending nuclear holocaust as an ineffable or unknowable science-fiction element, such as the Zone, is not exactly cutting-edge. Postwar science-fiction films are endlessly cluttered with these tropes, and while this *is* always present and evident within Tarkovsky's film, one would like to imagine, given his immensity as an artist and span of vision, that there was more going on here than a simple illumination of nuclear terror. While Tarkovsky may have felt the mystic geography of his film was more incidental than substantial, and since he did have to sporadically change filming location, one could imagine his feelings towards the outward appearance of the Zone to be far from objective. It's hard to agree with that, especially when the landscape of the film so unequivocally connects as essential to the plot of the film, and the elements of its landscape, insofar as they are encountered, perfectly encapsulate the emotions of the given moment, and often, in a literal, functioning way, a performative utilization of its offering. Consider another film, Denis Villeneuve's *Arrival* (2016), where the protagonists must communicate with the visiting alien heptapods through their ship, in a large room—between them is a large plexiglass-like border, through which they communicate by drawing with large black markers. In the dim setting of that room takes place the most informational and interesting scenes in the film. If it instead offered us a bright, neon alien environment for these transactions, it would be a very different setup for the film, and ultimately, an atmospherically unsatisfying payoff. The atmosphere and aesthetic are very specific, from the hauntingly sparse soundtrack to the large recurrent of water slightly dripping, to the full-on sensation of drowning. All of which is very incumbent to the influence of *Stalker*.

There's even a scene in the film with snow falling in the summer and white foam floating down the river. In fact, it was the chemical that made the water appear opaque. The water shots are always fascinating because of the artifacts we see scattered under the water in various shots; various unclassifiable rubles and other coins, a small World War 2-era sub-machine gun, a close-up of Writer's gun as Stalker

A fraction of the Ghent Altarpiece. © Mosfilm

kicks it into the water. We get a nice shot of the dismantled bomb with some eel-like fish swimming above it. Most significantly, during the Stalker's dream sequence earlier in the film, we see some other rubles and coins, as well as a fractured piece of *The Ghent Altarpiece*, also known as the *Adoration of the Mystic Lamb*, an enormous 15th-century polyptych altarpiece by two early Flemish painters Jan and Hubert van Eyck.

After the whole sordid affair in the Zone is over, we return once again to the bar, where the three men drink in silence with their new canine companion, the dog from the Zone. Stalker's Wife enters and after a quick chat—asks about the dog, informs him his Daughter is waiting outside—they depart the bar. We get a final shot of the Writer and the Professor and then shots of Stalker, his Wife and Daughter, walking along a tiny beach beside a lake (or some other water-structure: too small for ocean, too large for creek-bed.) Across from them: a huge nuclear powerplant. Apparently, this was the moment in the film of greatest importance to Tarkovsky. In an interview from 1980 with Luisa Capo, he said: '...The one [scene] closest to my heart is... let's say the one I feel as my own and in which I have perhaps expressed myself to the fullest. It is probably one of the final scenes, beginning with their return to the bar and home, up until the conversation with the wife. When everything is in the past already.' The scene curiously, features a return to color, once we are outside the bar, something that was only seen within the Zone. Why? What does this symbolize? The technology presented to us is a devastating one, the one that—potentially—left the Zone so ravaged, perhaps the cause of all of Stalker and his family's ailments. This could be an insight. Alternatively, if you take the position that the Zone is real, then the nuclear presence stands easily as a grotesque manifestation of the unnatural world, of humanity gone so badly awry that it has premeditated its own undoing. Either way, it's a predicative statement, against war machines, against totalitarianism and shows Stalker and his family, their whole lives becoming tiny dots, insignificant when weighed against the enormity of the nuclear structure. When we're still in close with Stalker and his family, before the camera pans out, there's a sense of an unspeakable intimacy. The characters are not speaking, simply enjoying being together once more. Stalker is definitely irreversibly traumatized from this latest trip into the Zone, but there's a sense of something else as well, of an ending, and indeed, back at the apartment he declares that he intends not to take any more clients into the Zone. When we do return to the apartment, the film returns to sepia, which gives it all a strange dreamlike sensation, like the Zone was a thing that happened long ago, elsewhere, maybe in some other film.

Was the Zone, in fact, real? Jacques Derrida in *Right of Inspection* says that the dilemma of narrative is that the inherent desire to ascribe narrative is not necessarily entirely insurmountable, but is 'practically innumerable', in its varieties and therein that convention controls the unfolding of narrative, because the audience is incapable of submitting to the behest of their gaze. At the end of the day we *can't know* due to its—and by extension the Room's—metaphysical open-endedness. We will never know, leaving the film with a deeply human feeling and an uncertainty. But in the best way possible, it's just that.

Endnotes

8. Fantasmatic (Phantasmatic): Relating to or of the nature of a phantasm; phantasmal, incorporeal, illusory. In Lacanian analytical terms, it refers not simply to what is fantastical or illusionary but insofar as narrative it poses how we can attempt to understand an unknowable Otherness.
9. Anthropocene: the current historical epoch, the age of human dominance over nature through ecologically consumptive forms of governance, e.g. global deforestation.
10. It's worth acknowledging that David Lynch's first film *Eraserhead* (1977) was actually released two years before *Stalker*, so he was well on his way. Lynch is surprisingly not actually on record citing Tarkovsky as a direct influence, but it's not hard to see—in the continuation of *Twin Peaks* from 2017, a trio of characters visit a portal to another dimension known as 'The Zone'. It's difficult not to assume.
11. Indices—as utilized by Deleuze is defined as: a sensory apparatus, which acts like a synecdoche for something of interest. E.g. Gunsmoke indicates gunfire, crying indicates sorrow.
12. Comparisons to Plato's Cave seem somewhat a stand-in for anything with subtext that intertextually depicts someone interacting with others showing cynicism. To me, it's a pointless comparison to make. In a general sense, however, it is very easy to look at *Stalker* in platonic terms—if one thinks of the film as a text where one has philosophy and poetry side-by-side. As Tarkovsky often said, true poets are always philosophers and vice-versa.
13. According to *USA Today*, an estimated 150 to 200 people called самосёлы/Samosely reside still in the Chernobyl Exclusion Zone. These are all former residents who refused to evacuate after the disaster. In the past 25 years there have been more than 900 deaths and just one birth. The average age of the Samosely or 'self-settlers' is 63, and they receive aggressively limited social support from the Belarus and Ukrainian governments.

The Aesthetics of *Stalker*

'Everything will begin to reverberate in response to the dominant note: things, landscape, actors' intonation. It will all become interconnected and necessary. One thing will be echoed by another in a kind of general interchange: and an atmosphere will come into being as a result of this concentration on what is most important. [...] It seems to me that in *Stalker*, where I tried to concentrate on what was most important, the atmosphere that came to exist as a result was more active and emotionally compelling than that of any of the films I had made previously.' – Andrei Tarkovsky, Sculpting in Time (1986: 194)

© Daisy Braun

Tarkovsky's style is highly original, which is probably one of the most utterly enjoyable facets of watching his films. His cinematography (with respect to Aleksandr Knyazhinsky, the principal cinematographer for *Stalker*) is intensely deliberate and often his shots appear more akin to compositional renderings of paintings than settings for a drama. His eye for the elements of cinema is arguably unrivaled in the history of filmmaking. The aesthetics of *Stalker* fall all over the board, at times vastly differing from what you'd expect of the film thematically, which can come off as utterly surprising as a viewer, but in the best way, expanding the depths of the film incrementally with its bold palette choices and themes. If one agrees with Theodor Adorno, who writes in *Aesthetic Theory* that the darkening of the world begets the rationalizing of the irrationality of art, which begets a radically darkened art (19), then it becomes very riveting to engage with *Stalker* a film so utterly tied to the anthropological darkness of the nuclear era.

Anti-Oz: Color and Noncolor

Color is so, so important in *Stalker*—as focused and deliberate in its use (and, its lack) as some of the greatest films related to color in cinema: Kieslowski's *Three Colours* films (1993–94), Wong Kar-wai's *In the Mood for Love* (2000), the films of Peter Greenaway, and certainly *The Wizard of Oz*. If we view the world as it is seen in the film, it is a harsh place, monochromatic, sepia; dehydrated and desolate... then, we receive the vibrancy of the Zone, which we must interpret as all the more alarming and wondrous for its alarmingly bright receptivity. The delineation of color and noncolor throughout the film is one of the most distinct characterizations of his films, literally, one of the traits that has come to revered under the umbrella term of Tarkovskian. All of his feature films save his first, *Ivan's Childhood*, appear in color, with black-and-white or sepia sequences in the mix, typically as dream sequences, video recordings or flashbacks. Tarkovsky knows how to utilize color quite well. He understands its dilemmas: 'One of the greatest difficulties in the graphic realization of a film is, of course, colour' (138). Tarkovsky, particularly during the period of *The Mirror* and *Stalker* seemed to view color more as conditional to the financial success of the films of the era, as he says: 'At present colour is less a question of aesthetics than of commercial necessity' (138), as opposed to an artistic distinction, which is likely largely factored into his then-determination to use color in an unorthodox or contrarian manner. He does at least in part seem to view color in film as a capital-driven choice for much of his career, even in later years.

The trio in the film's most famous scene. © Mosfilm

Stalker opens in a dusty palette of the world outside of the Zone: a high contrast sepia that in certain dark rooms, makes you strain your eyes to try and catch the details on screen. The noncolor perfectly matches the tone the film conveys in its opening sequences—lethargic, wearisome, carceral and stressed. Of course, the dullness is distinctive from NO color; not a black-and-white. Sagacity as opposed to downright melancholy. The sepia often collocates together a lot of light browns and ugly shades of yellow colors, which gives the outer-world of *Stalker* a very sickly atmosphere; this world, we can tell very clearly, is unwell. The compositions of the opening shots are lethargic and very deliberate as well—shots of the bar in the opening and subsequent departure scenes are extremely symmetrical; as well as the shots of Stalker's apartment, almost like paintings.

Then, in the dull monochrome of this world, we have the three men on the trolley-car—backed by a steady sound of clanking metal, momentarily met with some jolting synths, soundtracking them on the way. The film focuses in on the face of each man—Writer, Professor, Stalker, very, very slowly so we witness the full range of emotions they're feeling in the moment. Then, as if no time has passed at all, suddenly, we are in, and it's an unnerving moment. Like a weirdly Uncanny Valley moment; an anti-*Wizard of Oz*; the film has turned entirely full-color. But without the joy of a yellow-brick road, this space is dangerous. The journey—this initial beginning and further developments—will be exhausting, emotionally and otherwise. When we emerge into the blindingly ultra-vivid scene of the Zone, we are met with a few telephone poles, disconnected but clear, as a somewhat blaring religious iconoclast, greeting us in the land of faith. At this moment there are three of them, three men, embarking into the Zone, and cross-like poles, which is not lost on us as an audience. Beyond the religious iconography the erosion—forced or otherwise—of invasive humanity from the natural world, and its subsequent regrowth, or overgrowth into a new manifested-Thing. And the coloring of this thing is overwhelmingly bright.

When Tarkovsky writes on color in his film theory book *Sculpting in Time*, he seems to be speaking very directly of the style choices made specifically for *Stalker*, the contrast of color with noncolor and its deliberate emphasis to highlight the negation:

> The perception of colour is a physiological and psychological phenomenon to which, as a rule, nobody pays particular attention. [...] You have to try and neutralize colour, to modify its impact on the audience. If colour becomes the dominant dramatic element of the shot, it means that the director and cameraman are using a painter's methods to affect the audience. That is why nowadays one very often finds that the average expertly made film will have the same sort of appeal as the luxuriously illustrated glossy magazine; the colour photography will be warring against the expressiveness of the image. Perhaps the effect of colour should be neutralized by alternating colour and monochrome sequences, so that the impression made by the complete spectrum is spaced out, toned down. Why is it, when all that the camera is doing is recording real life on film, that a coloured shot should seem so unbelievably, monstrously false? The explanation must surely be that colour, reproduced mechanically, lacks the touch of the artist's hand; in this area he loses his organizing function, and has no means of selecting what he wants (138).

He seems wary of instilling images on the screen that could appear at all fake or untrustworthy to the audience, but also seems to acknowledge the inevitability of color technologically. It seems to some extent he is not speaking to his own cinema but focused more on bemoaning the state of decay in modern film, inasmuch as he references the idea that *nowadays* one finds even expertly made films warring against their nature, against their expressive qualities. He seems to be working against these kinds of abstractions for the remainder of his career, fighting to evoke breathtaking and extreme emotionality from a form that he is partially distrustful of. Tarkovsky is no stranger to these techniques of use-of-color mixed with black-and-white imagery. His incredible second feature film *Andrei Rublev* (which *The Guardian* recently credited as the greatest arthouse film of all time), shows his keen desire to cast an atmospheric effect with sudden use of color. Unlike *Stalker* which uses its colorization dramatically to full effect with the emerging Zone—and again in and out of color at the end of the film—*Andrei Rublev* takes a subtler approach, akin to the minimal-but-poigant use of color in a film like *Rumble Fish* (1983) or *Battleship Potemkin* (1925). *Andrei Rublev* follows the historical and personal life of its titular lead, Andrei Rublev, a famous 15th-century Russian painter, and saint, who was canonized by the Russian Orthodox Church in 1988, likely due in some part to Tarkovsky's film preserving his legacy. The film was shot on black-and-white film, except for its final sequence: the film highlights Rublev's beautifully painted biblical pieces, then a crossfade to four horses grazing in the distance; the image of the horse operates as a synecdoche throughout the film for nature, moreover for the brutality of human cruelty against nature, against itself too. Showing the world in color helps cement its permanence in history: Rublev overcoming his suppressors, conquering the hardships, surviving it all. Glorious and lavish as that sounds—and indeed, visually, it certainly is to behold—it's only 9 minutes of color, less than 4 percent of the entire film's length, at 205 minutes. The grueling length of the film brings the audience to the color sequence already emotionally exhausted and therein the colored section showcasing his religious iconography all the more breathtaking to see in full color.

Between *Andrei Rublev* and *Stalker* Tarkovsky made two films which both utilized transitions between full color and black-and-white footage: *Solaris* and the *The Mirror*. *The Mirror* is his most biographical film, and operates as vaguely nonlinear in its narrative, with flashbacks and long poetry readings. For this, the transitional abruptions of color-to-noncolor are very effective in conveying the time-switch clearly, clarifying what might otherwise be confusing in transition, since it is so stream-of-consciousness at times. All seven of his feature films use color in different and intriguing ways. *Solaris* really pushes the limits on satiating its palettes, with color sequences ranging from black-and-white—the famous sequence when the retired pilot Berton drives through a future Tokyo, mostly through dark tunnels. The film's main setting, the space station, is so beautifully colored and profoundly of its era—the visuals remain with you forever. Notable also is the bright lively natural tones of the beginning of the film, when Kelvin visits at his father's house, especially in contrast to the end of the film, when the planet Solaris generates an artificial reconstruction of that same setting but everything is dead, frozen and cold. The film also features some wonderful scenes in blue, and red tints.

We must mention Fleming's *The Wizard of Oz*, released in 1939. No film aside perhaps from *Stalker* can rival its significance in regard to that expert turn from noncolor to color in film; when Dorothy cracks the door open and steps into Technicolor, into Oz, for the first time. From this moment, even the most cynical critic, skeptical of the 'gimmick' of it, is going to feel *something*. When the average American viewer saw *The Wizard of Oz* for the first time in the years after 1939 they were totally denied the effect—since most television units at the time were still in black-and-white—but for those who saw the film as intended, then and since, the message is clear: the Technicolor is a firm catalyst of the wonderment of the film. Such is obviously the case for *Stalker* as well but not without an additional air of unease—the Zone is luscious, its green, the brightest green, ripe and magnificent, but also deathly still; there's no people here, it is unlike Oz in the eeriness of its conditions.

A film that demonstrates a mastery of color and palette, with the same proficiency as *Stalker* is Bergman's *Viskningar och rop/Cries and Whispers* (1972). The film is overwhelming with its palette; sharply blinding crimson, complete with fadeouts where the entire screen turns red. All of the protagonists wear white, and the film juxtaposes these two colors aggressively throughout. The red emphasizes the film's continued focus on lust, passion and fever. While the film could not be psychically further from *Stalker*—it is a film about terminality, suffering, familial bond and abandonment, and female sexuality. None of these themes bears much relevance to the goings on in Tarkovsky's film, but they are similar too. The film opens with a shot of the terminally ill Agnes, who awakens, parched. She very slowly takes a drink of water and it seems to sit poorly in her throat. The shot is just like the opening of *Stalker*, when, almost compositionally, we receive Stalker from above, lying in bed, staring up, looking over at his Daughter and Wife, and then sliding out of bed. The color scheme couldn't be further from the eye-candy of blaring crimsons of Bergman's film; this is the heart of Tarkovsky's sepia browns after all, but the shots are so similar, both intimately allowing us interconnection with the respective protagonists, experiencing their intimate inner aesthetics with them—the world of their bedsides, their awakenings. Again, compositionally, the films couldn't be more alike.[14]

Aside from *The Wizard of Oz*, the most famous cinema relation to color comes from Kieslowski. Kieslowski's *Trois Couleurs/Three Colours* Trilogy is a series of three films, released in 1993 and 1994, each separate but uniquely linked in their focus on being shot primarily with a single color as its center-focus, *Bleu/Blue* (1993), *Blanc/White* (1994), and *Rouge/Red* (1994) respectively. These colors are chosen specifically to match the Three Ideals of the French revolutionaries and indeed, the colors of the *Tricolore* the French Flag. Kieslowski is super dedicated to the formal experimentation of his films—his masterpiece is certainly his other grand experiment, the ten-piece television drama *Dekalog* (1989), where each hour is dedicated to modernizing one each of the Ten Commandments. Kieslowski's films never feel kitschy, the color incorporation is always earnest, and not just adding to the tone of the film, but immensely defining what the tone will be for the film. What helps is the brutal self-awareness: many refer to and interpret the *Three Colours* films as anti-tragedy, always self-aware in spite of their own conformity to a dramatic narrative. But, the color is always sincere, just like the colors of the Zone in *Stalker*, though of course, in contrast to those films, *Stalker*'s colors are often subdued, dull and uninhibited (save for the lush greenery of the Zone). Like Tarkovsky, Kieslowski uses—and refrains from using—color with such a deliberateness that even though one watches his films with the knowledge that the very pathos of the film is the color scheme, it still manages to stick out as remarkable in apropos of its deliberate aesthetic.

Tarkovsky's careful and brilliant usage of color starts with his first films shot in color, *Solaris* and *The Mirror*, and of course, the ending to *Andrei Rublev*. In 1966, concurrent with the December release of *Andrei Rublev*, Tarkovsky gave an interview to Maria Chugunova (who would go on to become his assistant director for *Solaris*, *Mirror*, and *Stalker*) where he gave insight on his disdain for color in film, foreshadowing perhaps his more selective, deliberate usages of color in his next films:

> For the moment I don't think colour film is anything more than a commercial gimmick. [...] In any film the graphics impinge on one's perception of the events. In everyday life we seldom pay any special attention to colour. When we watch something going on we don't notice colour. A black-and-white film immediately creates the impression that your attention is concentrated on what is most important. [...] Colour film as a concept uses the aesthetic of principles of painting or colour photography. As soon as you have a colour picture in the frame it becomes a moving painting. It's all too beautiful, and unlike life. What you see in cinema is a coloured, painted plane, a composition on a plane. In a black-and-white film there is no feeling of something extraneous going on, the audience can watch the film without being distracted from the action by colour (356).

When he speaks of 'the moment you start to notice it', though this interview takes place more than a decade prior to *Stalker*, it still feels paramount to the beautiful transitional moment when the trio enter the Zone and spring to life with color. It speaks well to the moment in *Andrei Rublev* where the color is shown as well. If it weren't such a stark transition, one might not be compelled to even notice it, which is what makes the color so dazzling in its suddenness; which is definitely the point Tarkovsky is trying to make in this interview. Notice also how Tarkovksy seems keen on controlling color so completely in his cinema—it seems almost as if he'd rather shoot in black-and-white than to have color that distracts from his composition, or more, becomes disingenuous to the vision of it. This is confirmed by Chugunova, years later when she herself is interviewed about working on *Stalker* as the assistant director, by legendary Russian film critic Maya Turovskaya for her 1991 book *7½*

Films of Andrei Tarkovsky. Chugunova says: '[...] If there were ten twigs on a tree, Andrei Arsenevich would check each and every one of them to see how it looked in the scene: perhaps it should be cut off or lengthened, add some silver here or brown there, or cover the trunk with soot to make it blacker and more interesting — everything was always brought to the condition he needed.' We know Tarkovsky to be an extremely detail-oriented director in many aspects of his filmmaking, aesthetic no exception. The idea that he would concern himself with something as relatively miniscule as the coloring of a tree-trunk or the number of branches in the foreground might seem like a trivial exaggeration for effect, but when one examines just how explicitly careful each compositional shot is in *Stalker* (among all his films, really), it becomes quite sensible. There are so many intricate details to pick up in the film. A few to note: in the scene when the motorcyclist just misses the trio driving away, the initials *A.K.* can just barely be seen carved into a wall in the street on the left side of the screen. Tarkovsky inserted this as a subtle homage to Akira Kurosawa. Additionally, twice in the film the initials *AT* can be seen; first on the helmet of that same police officer on the motorcycle and then the pack of cigarettes that Stalker's wife smokes from. These initials are Tarkovsky's. There is subtlety in color and tone usage as well.

The noncolor-to-color-to-noncolor contrast comes to mind as most visually pressing in the film. The grimly monochrome tone of the world outside of the Zone feels all the sicklier next to the almost feverishly lush greenery of the Zone. The significance always for Tarkovsky here, seems to come with the transition. He speaks of this again and again in interviews whenever the topic of color in cinema is raised, his intention to utilize color and black-and-white in his films, push against the limitations of the medium while doing so. Later in the Turovskaya interview, Chugunova recalls the director's focus on color in *Stalker*:

> He needed image that was sort of on the one hand in colour and on the other — without colour. Or he would like an image with only one colour detail: for example, everything in black and white but the face looking natural and he'd like to do it not by combining shots but to photograph it that way. Of course, our technology had not reached that level yet. But there is one such close-up of Grinko [Professor] asleep in *Stalker*. More or less like the entire *Sacrifice*: earthy; Nykvist [Sven

Nykvist, Swedish cinematographer on *The Sacrifice*] has captured it brilliantly.

Photography is an interesting word to bring into play regarding the cinematography of the film. I'm thinking of Roland Barthes and the idea that the photograph reproduces in perpetuity what has only happened in reality a single time: that the photograph mechanically—functionally—repeats what could never be repeated existentially. That's the power of the breathless still shots in *Stalker*. With the exception of a few memorable moments in the innermost parts of the Zone, almost all of these shots are—when void of context—entirely ordinary: establishing shot in the bar, in the apartment, and of the three travelers resting in the Zone. The latter, most ordinate of all; close-ups of the three men simply sleeping, their faces motionless, like the one referenced by Chugunova of The Professor. It's not the gravity of the narrative nor the weight of the character development that makes these images so evocative, that is, repeats what *could* perhaps be recreated existentially, but it is the infinite beauty of a still that depicts something of interminable ardor. For Tarkovsky, who was making a film about intense faith, nothing could be more essential. Additionally, to bring in the context, these arcadian images of the men sleeping in the overgrowth of nature ready to swallow them whole at any second, is extraordinarily powerful. When you add in, what we know of the Zone—its potential levels of radioactivity, its fantasmatic factors, it gives the viewer an immense sense of unease and anxiety to see the men so unarmed in unconsciousness. And Stalker's dream sequence—which returns us momentarily to sepia—is also equal parts silently beautiful and startlingly discomforting.

Few film directors seem ready to attempt these sorts of emotional transition to-and-from color as boldly as Tarkovsky or Fleming do; it's a risky technique, that can come off as kitschy as it does emotionally rewarding in *Stalker*. In general, subtlety is more often and favorably conceived with the inclusion of both; films like *Rumble Fish* and *Andrei Rublev* that linger on the conservative side with their color usage to great effect. No color-inclusion is perhaps more important or more emotionally satisfying than the other great Russian film to utilize color, Sergei Eisenstein's 1925 film *Battleship Potemkin*. The film chronicles the mutiny of the titular battleship—at the end, the rebels raise a red flag to signal their success on the ship, but since the film was shot with a black-and-white film stock, it appeared black on screen. For the film's

The opening shot to the second half of Stalker. © *Mosfilm*

premiere at the Grand Theater in Moscow, Eisenstein laboriously hand-tinted the film himself, for 108 frames with red dye, so that the flag would appear red.

When the flag showed on screen, the Bolsheviks in the audience were exhilarated and Eisenstein received a standing ovation. The effect of the colorization needs no explanation here—like *Stalker* it pulls you into a new world of realism, magical or otherwise. Though, incidentally, Tarkovsky was no fan of Eisenstein, writing in his diaries that he was 'radically opposed' to Eisenstein's cinematographic style, his use of the frame as a means to an end to intellectualize his ideas purely; Tarkovsky refutes this as propagandist, insisting his cinema strive for 'deeply intimate experience', arguing that Eisenstein's film style lacked the unsaid element of mystery, the element of cinema that allows one to project oneself to empathize with the narrative (183-184). I think Tarkovsky underestimates film viewers here, however: perhaps one does not need to identify with the curated film aesthetics or narrative arcs of cinema to engage with them successfully. This must be true at least for the appreciation of Eisenstein's films, or, as my colleague Devin Snell says of the film, 'to experience meaningfully interaction with art in a word piloted by evil men'. Certainly, this is necessary in contemporary cinema, where otherwise enjoyable autobiographical films produced by filmmakers with problematic histories who one would never wish to 'relate with' in any conceivable form.

Meaning and Time

Directing attention to the looming colorless and curious character of the Dog: the dog (to distinguish from the character of the Dog) who was chosen to portray the Dog, was a local Estonian sheepdog who was reportedly extraordinarily well-trained, very obedient and would lie down in the stream beside the Stalker for as long as commanded. The Dog should be treated as one of the more examinable icons in the film, particularly notable for their distinct lack of color in the world that is so essentially full of greenery and blues and whites. The curious animal only makes a few major appearances in the film, and it has been speculated on as having all sorts of significance—from being The Black Dog, the Welsh portent of death and an evil foreboding omen of death, to the exact opposite: a loving representation of loyalty, friendship and adoration for mankind, qualities the Stalker is said to possess. One turns to Tarkovsky, who yields us contradiction; he famously dismisses the constant yearning for interpretive looks at *Stalker*: 'People always try to find hidden meanings in my films. But wouldn't it be strange to make a film while striving to hide one's thoughts? My images do not signify anything beyond what they are' (72). But, he also includes lot of mythic and interpretable elements in his films that *must* be seen as such—some critics agree that portions of the dream sequence in *The Mirror* are directly reminiscent of the Japanese mythos of the Yūrei, a ghost-like specter. The most fascinating thing regarding the Dog in *Stalker* is his presence after their return from the Zone. His being there, coincides with the strange return-to-color, even after they've returned. This is the first time we see this outside the Zone, any vibrance, and it's unclear why that it is, and indeed, if it somehow pertains to this Dog. A common thought might be to give the Dog some sort of credit or spiritual, literary importance: they represent the Stalker in some way, perhaps, or an embodiment of whatever element of the Zone. This may not be the case though, and the Dog is simply a harmless creature, who happened to reside in the Zone. He has so much resonance to us, and perhaps he does symbolize *something* for Stalker, but he himself being harmless makes him more intriguing than any alternative, a double-set up. If the Dog was a simple omen of death or negativity in the Zone, that would be effective but far less interesting. When the three men return from the Zone, the Dog comes with them, and subsequently follows Stalker and his family to their home. In their kitchen, Stalker's Wife pours some milk from a bag for the Dog who laps it up excitedly, as if they perhaps have not had anything to drink in a long time.

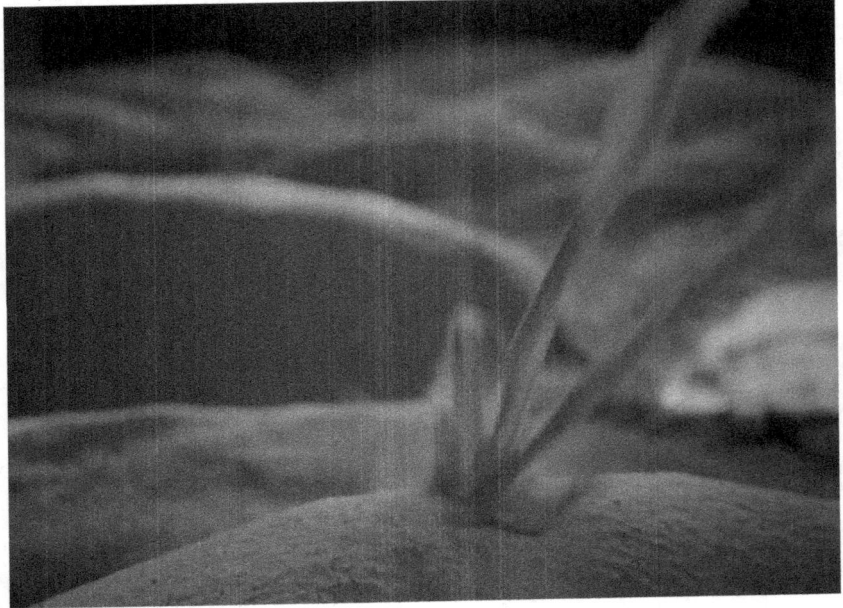

The metal nut ricochets with the sand dune. © Mosfilm

A lot of these allusions and cryptic symbolism feel intentional and decipherable. Occasionally, there is something that is perhaps, *just so*. Notably, the strips of cloth tied to the metal nuts, that the trio throw in various locations as a safety precaution. The items are fascinating to look at but in all likelihood are just utility-themed; there's nothing deep or compelling about the objects. When Stalker throws the final one in the film—in the room with the barchan sand dunes where Writer has gone ahead—we watch as the metal bolt hit a crescent-dune and plummets upwards, then ricochets off into the distance. It's a gorgeous shot; but is just pure aesthetic. That said, these are the kinds of shots that are gorgeous and rewarding to appreciate. Tarkovsky has lots of deliberate and unconscious allusions; though he actively attempted to never emulate other artists, he acknowledged its inevitability and even pointed some of them out:

> ...In *The Mirror* for instance, there are two or three shots that are very clearly inspired by Brueghel: the boy, the small silhouettes of men, the snow, the bare trees, and the river in the distance. I created these shots very consciously and deliberately, not with the idea of copying or to show culture but to bear witness to my love for Brueghel, of my dependence on him, of the deep impression that he has made on my life. In *Andrei Rublev*, there was a scene that might have been from Mizoguchi, the great departed Japanese director... It's the one where the Russian prince gallops across the countryside on a white horse, and the Tatar is on a black horse. [...] The two riders gallop after each other. Suddenly the Tatar cries out, whistles, whips his horse, and overtakes the prince. The Russian goes after him but cannot catch up. In the next shot, they have stopped. [...] It's a scene that has nothing to do with the plot of the story. It attempts to express the state of a soul and to throw light on the nature of the relationship between two men (53-54).

In *Stalker* when the Stalker speaks of pliancy and weakness, this is actually neither he nor Tarkovsky speaking at all: 'Pliancy and weakness are signs of the freshness of being' was an epigraph Tarkovsky read in the novel *Pamphalon The Mountebank* by the Russian author Nikolai Leskov, who himself borrowed it from the ancient Chinese philosopher Lao-Tzu. The film is bursting with Taoist philosophy, a dignified religion that itself centers around three 'treasures', a tripartite ethos of frugality, humility, and compassion.

Stalker is certainly a film open to a vast array of interpretive analysis, and while Tarkovsky himself seems adamant that the film is a hopeful one, towards a radical statement on human dignity or love, it's difficult to not become dissuaded of this, by the unrelentingly nihilistic moments of the film, the deep dark trenches of its setting;

while the Zone is lush, it's deadly. And the world outside it, no better. Deleuze in *The Time-Image* speaks about crystal-image, derived from Bergson's writings on duration. To examine crystal-image in Tarkovsky we should understand its purpose in Deleuze's cinematic trajectory. Deleuze's crystal-image is a delineation in film that depicts how the characters maneuver through time and space. Crystal-image is a stand-in for splitting in time, the move from the past to the present, as seen through the images projected on the screen, the 'uniting of an actual image and virtual image to the point where they can no longer be distinguished' (335). Deleuze insists that film seeks to provide bigger circuits to link actual imagery with the human experience of the past. This is Deleuze's exposition of time in cinema, though the purest form of crystal-image is the manner in which we exist in time. Deleuze writes on *Solaris* and *Stalker*:

> ...Are we to believe that the soft planet Solaris gives a reply, and that it will reconcile the ocean and thought, the environment and the seed, at once designating the transparent face of the crystal (the rediscovered woman) and the crystallizable form of the universe (the rediscovered dwelling)? *Solaris* does not open up this optimism, and *Stalker* returns the environment to the opacity of an indeterminate zone, and the seed to the morbidity of something aborting, a closed door. [...] In the crystal-image there is this mutual search – blind and halting – of matter and spirit: beyond the movement-image, 'in which we are still pious' (75).

Faith

Of course, in purest construct, the concept of faith is certainly not something one would want to adhere as aesthetical, in hopes of not insulting any true believers among one's audiences. That said, it would simply be naïve to ignore that aspect of *Stalker*. Tarkovsky's religion—while certainly debatable in its own right—is by any account, extremely important to his filmmaking. He is at the very least extremely interested in the notion of a true believer, and perhaps Russian orthodoxy is not exactly a category for the man or his films, but the iconography throughout *Stalker* certainly showcases a director who, at the very least, has a keen awareness of the important undercutting connection between faith and survival in unrelentingly cruel conditions.

A large visual inspiration of Tarkovsky's for *Stalker*, according to his protégé and then-intern Arvo Iho, was the works of French baroque painter Frances Poussin: 'Strange as it may sound, with 'Stalker' the French painter Nicolas Poussin (1594-1665) was taken as a model. Poussin's paintings frequently have mythological subjects and in principle 'Stalker' is also based on a myth. On faith.' Faith is the key here; Poussin's work while varied is always very theological. Composition is also the easiest influence to see from the baroques for Tarkovsky; his shots are always extremely intentional, recurring and symmetrical. Interestingly, Poussin twice portrays the scriptural story of *The Road to Emmaus* where two unsuspecting Christians encounter and are then led by a resurrected Christ. We know Tarkovsky was very inspired by *Emmaus* for making *Stalker*. The trio of travelers en-route to their destination is an obvious parallel.

Writer wearing his faux crown of thorns. © Mosfilm

Tarkovsky is no foreigner to the mending of art and divinity in film—in his second feature, *Andrei Rublev*'s titular Rublev spends his entire life musing on the conjunction and synchronicity between sublimity in art and in faith. Rublev ultimately seems to come to terms at the end of his life with this struggle. Faith in *Stalker* is not so linear, particularly because our protagonists are not so devout as Andrei Rublev is. Even Stalker himself, who is certainly acolyte in service to the Room in the Zone, seems to falter in his services to the place, declaring near the end of the film that he no longer intends to lead others to the place.

Faith-acts in *Stalker* are always gilded in irrationality, this is very intentional. We get the Professor, determined to blow up the Room; we have endless actions from Stalker beyond the realm of reasonability, all justified by his faith. The irrational nature of the faith-act annunciates to us its incredulousness, which gives it a more filmic quality, certainly; but also helps illuminate the true gravity of 'the leap' of the faith.

Various scholarly interpretations give the Zone all sorts of symbolism—a Mecca that can often come across as more spiritual or phenomenological than purely operating in the realms of science-fiction. This is not, though, a 'magical' place, where things just happen; everything is very purposeful. When the Zone shifts it does so with intention, to thwart the travelers' specific actions. As mentioned, for Tarkovsky, the plot—including the Zone—was always secondary to the envelopment of the characters in it. In interviews, he said regarding *Stalker*, that the plot interested him least, strictly speaking; the only fantastic element [for him] was simply the film's point of departure, nothing more.

Sounds and Sound of Silence

Equal to the striking visuals of *Stalker* are its sound choices, and—I cannot stress this enough—its unequivocal silences. While it is dialogue-heavy as a film—especially for Tarkovsky—the film is packed with moments of unconscious breath-holding, when the silence permeates; enhances a breathtaking shot or sequence's delicate composition with its auditory omissions. Silence in cinema is a painfully underused element, especially in genre films.

Before we examine silence metaphysically as it appears in the film, first, let's distinguish the literal acoustics of silence in its forms that Tarkovsky utilizes for *Stalker*.[15] Tarkovsky and Eduard Artemyev employ three types of silence: impressionist silence, diegetic absolute silence and, more briefly, non-diegetic absolute silence. Diegetic absolute silence is a silence generate by the negation of sound picked up by on-set equipment, with no added diegetic or non-diegetic sound. Meaning there is only the natural sound of the room's silence. Non-diegetic absolute silence is an unnatural silence—an intended muting of all sound, for the effect of deafness. This is used in film often after an extremely loud sound, like a bomb going off occurs, to simulate deafness—like the excellent scene when the protagonist's son, H.W. loses his hearing during a gas blowout in Paul Thomas Anderson's *There Will Be Blood* (2007)—it's more explicit and emboldened, whereas the former seems to be more often used to convey thematic tone or emotion. A good way to understand the metaphysical difference between the techniques is to think of them—to borrow from Sontag—the difference between *seeing* and *staring*. The third silence most commonly utilized in the film is impressionist silence (named for the impressionist film movement) and speaks to the blending of music/artificial sound into the silence to create an atmospherically noticeable quietness. The way that Stalker seems to relate to the Zone: finding himself at peace there in the silence, though it is *not* utterly silent.

Silence as aesthetic is complicated to say the least. Sontag describes it well in her much-read essay 'The Aesthetics of Silence':

> How literally can the notion of silence be used with respect to art? [...] Silence can't exist in a literal sense as the experience of an audience. It would mean that the spectator was aware of no stimulus or that he was unable to make a response. But this can't happen or be induced programmatically. The non-awareness of any stimulus, the inability to make a response, can result only from a defective presentness on the part of the spectator, or a misunderstanding of his own reactions (misled by restrictive ideas about what would be a 'relevant' response). But so far as any audience consists of sentient beings in a situation, there can be no such thing as having no response at all (6–7).

Silence can only exist as aesthetic in cinema—emphasizing the ascetic absence of desired sound or action, or harnessed, atmospherically creating a landscape, or as preemption. Silence cannot exist by itself, only insofar as it relates to, or negates from, the art. For Tarkovsky, the theoretical construction of absolute diegetic silence was overwhelming: 'The sounds of the world reproduced naturalistically in cinema are impossible to imagine: there would be a cacophony. [...] If there is no [sound] selection then the film is tantamount to silent, since it has no expression of its own' (159). He decries that natural diegetic as void of aesthetic content. Simultaneously—as evidenced in the infamous confrontation with composer Eduard Artemyev where he decided that the music for the tunnel sequence in *Stalker* was unnecessary—he does seem interested in the conveyance of film without music: 'I have to say in my heart of hearts I don't believe films need music at all,' he writes. 'I have not yet made a film without it, though I moved in that direction in *Stalker* and *Nostalghia*' (160). He goes on to state that, for cinematic image sound to be verified as truly genuine, it might mean the abandonment of music in film.

A key aspect of the film's make-up—echoing the essentiality of its sound design, silence, cinematography and coloring—is the soundtrack by Eduard Artemyev. Artemyev collaborated with Tarkovsky for *Solaris* and *Mirror*, and *Stalker* was their last project together, and the soundtrack's tones add an eerie finality to a film already plagued with an unsettling, haunted quality. The soundtrack blends (primarily) four sounds: a small sting orchestra, block flute, Synthi 100 synthesizer, and Artemyev also used a tar, a traditional Iranian stringed instrument, and attempted to mimic some forms of classic Indian music. The music for *Stalker* is quite transient and—all-in-total—only about 17 minutes of music, equal to less than 12 percent of the film's total run-time of almost 3 hours, though the primary theme does repeat a couple times, providing a tad bit more music for the film. Tarkovsky seems most interested in the use of electronic music on the soundtrack, and for film as a whole: 'Electronic music seems to me to have enormously rich possibilities for cinema' (161). And later: 'We wanted the sound to be close to that of an earthly echo, filled with poetic suggestion—to rustling, to sighing. The notes had to convey the fact that reality is conditional, and at the same time accurately to reproduce precise states of mind, the sounds of a person's interior world' (162).

In the scene when the trio first arrive in the Zone, Stalker briefly departs the other two to lie down in the grass, seemingly weak and exhausted by the return to his holy place. There is a natural organic silence to the scene, but also a generative sound, and even faintly, non-diegetic music which has been blended so seamlessly that it is almost unnoticeable, just like the sequence when the three first begin traveling to the Zone; where the rhythmic clanking of the railcar exists irrationally in synchronicity with the otherwise jarring sounds of synth music. This is a whole world away from the absolute diegetic silence, but it is a fascinatingly ideal utilization of sound in a film. The clanging of the train is the sound most commonly heard throughout the film—at least five times—either from Stalker's apartment, the bar or from inside the Zone. The sound easily serves as transitional, easing us to-and-from the world inside of the Zone, but also can be distinctly associated with Stalker himself traveling, as an audible motif of this illocutionary and atmospherically profound change of location.

Ode to Joy

Additionally, the film makes use of existing music—the film opens with a distant not-quite distinguishable recording of Beethoven's *Ninth Symphony*. Later, when the film transitions from the Zone outside the Room, back to the bar outside of it, we hear Ravel's *Boléro*, a one-movement crescendo that is slightly distorted as it is heard during zoom-in shots of Professor's dismantled bomb underwater; it is as if we are hearing the music from under the water. And, famously of course, as the film is concluding we hear a medley of familiar classic music all played at once as the train passes by—really the only piece we can identify is the loudest one, *Ode to Joy*, but there are traces of others there as well; Bizet, a quiet *Marseillaise*, the French national anthem, as well as perhaps Stravinsky. It is difficult to tell, it is all very quiet in comparison to the train. The chaotic noise—according to Artemyev—was supposed to correspond with the train as memory; the way one might remember fondly a piece of music from the radio associated in the mind as paired with the train sound. But more than anything else *Ode to Joy*.

How do we attempt to understand this? Beethoven's last great work is regarded for its incomprehensible emotional receptivity. This is—as Slavoj Žižek remarks in his analysis of the movement as an ideology—likely why factions as far ranging as the Nazis and the Bolsheviks, to the extreme Apartheidists in South Rhodesia and the European Union all have regarded the *Ninth Symphony* as their own anthem. To divulge slightly—the song comes from Beethoven at the end, his aesthetic intent to divert from normalcy. It's his 'late style' a phrase used to describe it by Adorno, which sees Beethoven composing *Ode to Joy* as a highly-revered veteran at the height of his craft, who steps away from communality within the society, the political culture—which he is irreducibly linked to—and contradicts it with a defiant counter-work. Adorno again, from an oft-cited fragmented essay on 'late style' Beethoven: '...The caesuras, the sudden discontinuities that more than anything else characterize the very late Beethoven, are those moments of breaking away; the work is silent at the instant when it is left behind, and it turns its emptiness outward.'[16] This contradicts a lot of what contemporary capitalist consumer culture would indicate to us about *Ode to Joy*. It's supposed to be *joyful*. It is, after all, in its originality, a German poem written by Friedrich Schiller about ideal humanity and romantic joy. And most of the time when it's used in cinema—and is it *ever*—it's done so in a tone-deaf romanticized fashion; *Dead Poets Society* (1989), *Sister Act* (1992), *Mr. Jones* (1993) and *Cruel Intentions* (1999), to name a few. It's an understandable aesthetic choice—the piece in its overwhelming emotionality resonates well in this manner.

So, what about a more intriguing usage of the piece? It's certainly less common but fascinating when it does occur.[17] The most famous depiction in film of *Ode to Joy* comes from Kubrick and *A Clockwork Orange* (1971). Beethoven's *Ninth Symphony* plays a crucial role in the film's narrative in general—first, we have Alex, our sadistic sociopathic antihero who is genuinely moved by the piece. Then, his traumatic torture conditioning—forced to endure footage of Nazi war crimes set to the *Ninth Symphony*—which renders the sound of that symphony as torturous and nauseating for him. But the *actual usage* of the music in the film is to fantastic effect: it is at once both joyous and terrifying, broadening the expanse of what the music itself should be able to generate in response from its audiences.

This is helpful to beginning to understand why it works as the concluding music for *Stalker*. A lesser film would suffer from its inclusion at the final scene—many have done so. Here, the film lives up to the artistic demands of the piece, irrefutably. It's most satisfying in its quality as open-ended—you can interpret it in the bleary authoritarianist all-is-lost way, or as a glimmer of actual joy, or hope. The inclusion of Beethoven's piece has specific symbolic implications that can be posed as political, ideological, or even religious. There is a teleological element to the sequence too, especially with the roar of industrialization, the triumph of modern society, but that subsequently becomes cacophonous and unrecognizable, as does the *Ninth Symphony*. What comes to mind here most prominently is Walter Benjamin, who writes at length in his notable essay 'The Work of Art in the Age of Mechanical Reproduction', on the consequences of changing productions/industrializations of art objects and how they are conveyed and received by the masses. Benjamin writes:

> Mechanical reproduction of art changes the reaction of the masses toward art. [...] With regard to the screen, the critical and the receptive attitudes of the public coincide. The decisive reason for this is that individual reactions are predetermined by the mass audience response they are about to produce, and this is nowhere more pronounced than in the film. The moment these responses become manifest they control each other. Again, the comparison with painting is fruitful. A painting has always had an excellent chance to be viewed by one person or by a few. The simultaneous contemplation of paintings by a large public, such as developed in the nineteenth century, is an early symptom of the crisis of painting, a crisis which was by no means occasioned exclusively by photography but rather in a relatively independent manner by the appeal of art works to the masses (234).

Tarkovsky's utilization of *Ode to Joy* transcends it's own contexts, forming new semiological meaning in the film. There is danger there, as Benjamin indicates, in audience misinterpretation. But also enormous potential in its new symbolisms.

For one thing, *Ode to Joy* is overwhelming—as a musical representative for all the ideologies potentially intended by Tarkovsky—and as a loud, powerful piece of music. It stands in such striking contrast to the diegetic and non-digetic absolute silences of the Zone. For the world outside the Zone, what better way to conclude with than a sound collage of noise—and best of all, a powerful anthemic piece, to illustrate the endless possibilities of Monkey's psychic moments which we see in those last four minutes of film, as the music plays out into the credits.

Endnotes

14. Interestingly, *Cries and Whispers* cinematographer Sven Nykvist (a frequent collaborator of Bergman) would go on to work with Tarkovsky for his final film, *The Sacrifice* in Sweden.

15. Phoebe Pua expertly analyzes Tarkovsky's use of all of these forms of silence and more in *Stalker* as well as *Nostalghia* and *The Sacrifice* in her delightful thesis 'Compositions of Crisis: Sound and Silence in the Films of Bergman and Tarkovsky'.
16. 'Late style' is a term coined by Adorno, whose last writings before his death were all for an imagined book on Beethoven. But the term goes back to an essay he began in 1937 on Beethoven's final compositions.
17. Further highlights on *Ode to Joy* used in an ideologically satisfying way: I'm sure most people are familiar with the usage of it in John McTiernan's film *Die Hard* (1988), which works very well during the penultimate climactic sequence where the terrorists have opened the vault and all is seemingly lost. Additionally, very movingly used in 新世紀エヴァンゲリオン/*Neon Genesis Evangelion* (1996); hummed by the character Kaworu Nagisa when first introduced as well as when he plunges to his death.

The Poetics of *Stalker* (Poetic Cinema)

'There are some aspects of human life that can only be faithfully represented through poetry.' -Andrei Tarkovsky, *Sculpting in Time* (1986: 30)

Andrei Tarkovsky is, in all regards, a cinematic auteur, credited with bringing poetic vision to the forefront of the film landscape. Rightfully so, his filmic constructions from *Ivan's Childhood* to *The Sacrifice*, seven films, all rife with what one could only attempt to describe accurately as 'poetic'. To attempt any other kind of cinematic interpretation without first acknowledging this would be conducting a gross injustice to the practically unreachable levels of achievement that Tarkovsky completes, perhaps none more so than with the opus, *Stalker*. Poetic cinema[18] is not an unusual classification for his films, although Tarkovsky himself would often bristle when it was suggested. He dismissed the label once, regarding the subgenre as unnecessary:

> No other art can compare with cinema in the form, precision and starkness with which it conveys awareness of facts and aesthetic structures existing and changing within time. I therefore find it particularly irritating the pretensions of modern 'poetic cinema', which involves breaking off contact with fact and with time realism and makes for preciousness and affectation (68-69).

Consequentially, even at his most poetically esoteric, Tarkovsky's films still dwell in a place mostly held aloft by narrative, or at the very least, narrative history. There is nothing in his films that could be called farfetched or self-servingly experimental, like the experimental sequence at the end of Kubrick's *2001: A Space Odyssey* (1968). It is worth acknowledging that Tarkovsky has no issue with the poetic cinema of the past, he speaks highly in interviews of Russian directors like Aleksandr Dovzhenko, Sergei Parajanov and Otar Iosseliani. Of the former he says: 'Dovzhenko the first director for whom the problem of atmosphere was particularly important' (21). Of the latter two: 'I regard [Iosseliani and Parajanov] as the best Soviet filmmakers' (69). It would be foolish to not admire these artists and the enormity of lyrics in their sometimes unclassifiable films, in the dialogue, cinematography and so on. How far afield is Tarkovsky in examining himself in this regard? Given the literal amount of poetry *within* the film, the term 'poetic cinema' does not feel so aloof a categorization for the film in this way. But both the poetics of the cinema itself, as well as his usage of (literal) poetry in his films is excellent, specifically in *Stalker*.

Parajanov, who Tarkovsky admired, was himself a much greater admirer of Tarkovsky, though Tarkovsky was in fact his junior by several years. Parajanov considered Tarkovsky his mentor, and he acknowledged in the documentary short *Andrei Tarkovsky & Sergei Paradjanov: Islands*, that his first viewing of Tarkovsky's first feature film *Ivan's Childhood* was instrumental in completely changing his artistic and poetic vision for aesthetics in cinema. Parajanov's greatest film *The Color of Pomegranates* (1965) is very invocative of Tarkovsky's film *Andrei Rublev*, as both films are grand tributes to ancient icons, Tarkovsky's to the titular painter of the 14th-century, Parajanov's the 18th-century poet Sayat Nova. The two men were so close that when Parajanov was indicted by the Soviets to a gulag for five years, for art trafficking and currency fraud, Tarkovsky wrote a letter to the Central Committee of the Communist Party of Ukraine, demanding the release of his friend, alongside some other artist friends—including Godard, Antonioni and the American author John Updike. Four years later Parajanov was released, one year early, in 1977, but lived in extreme poverty. Such was their friendship that Tarkovsky (according to a *Guardian* piece written on Parajanov by author Elif Batuman) went as far as to give Parajanov a prized antique ring to pawn, but Parajanov refused, keeping the ring instead, as a symbol of their friendship. Parajanov's last film, *Ashik Kerib* (1988) was an Azerbaijani folk tale, dedicated to Tarkovsky, who died two years previous. Both of these films—and Parajanov's other two films as well—are Tarkovskian films in their usage of poetry, and poetic movements in the surreal nonlinear experimentations of the films, particularly *Ashik Kerib* and his 1985 film *The Legend of the Surami Fortress* (1985).

Arseny Tarkovsky

In *Stalker*, during the journey to the Room in the Zone, there is a scene just prior to the appearance of the mysterious telephone, and after the room filled with barchans—the crescent-shaped sand dunes found most predominately in the area—just after the Writer has led the other two through what is posed as the most dangerous part of the Zone—the pipe known as the Meat Grinder. In this moment,

Stalker recalls a poem to his companions before approaching the Room:

> And now summer has left,
> as if it never came at all
> It's warm still where the sun falls
> But it's not enough.
>
> Whatever I wanted to happen
> fell right into my hands
> like a five-fingered leaf.
> But it is not enough.
>
> The just and unjust
> played their necessary part
> and burned into light.
> But it's not enough.
>
> Life tucked me behind its back
> and shielded me from cuffs.
> I've had such good luck
> But it's not enough.
>
> My leaves have yet to blasé;
> my branches have not yet broken.
> The day is clear as glass—
> But it's not enough.

The poem 'And now summer has left' was in fact, written by Tarkovsky's father Arseny Tarkovsky in 1967. The Stalker speaks the poem in the film;[19] he credits it to Porcupine's brother—Porcupine who mentored Stalker. Knowing that Arseny Tarkovsky is the true author of the poem suggests an interesting context, that this poem—within *Stalker* canon not the poem itself—is said to have been written by Porcupine's brother who we have just learned died in the same Meat Grinder they have just traversed. The poem is a curious choice—more despondent with the boredom of life than a meditation specific to the story. It does somewhat reflect on the character of Writer, who has made the journey to try and find inspiration and an end to his—for lack of a better term—apathy. Certainly, when a line is repeated from a poem in the film, it operates like a camera, focusing in, it has us leaning in, with heavier emphasis. In relation to the film, the cynicism of the poem clues us to the incoming inevitability that the Room in the Zone—which is said to grand the deepest desire of all who enter it—perhaps will not make the travelers as euphoric as they might be anticipating, this seems confirmed by the fate of Porcupine who hanged himself, after the Room failed to return his dead brother to life. The woeful, lethargic movement through the seasons in the poem (not all too unlike the other great Russian poets of the earliest twentieth century; poets like Osip Mandelstam, Sergei Yeltsin, and Vladimir Mayakovsky) carries the majority of the poem's emotional girth, and the not-quite-hoarse utterance from Stalker, equally conveys the poem's cynical forecast.

Stalker reciting the Arseny Tarkovsky poem. © Mosfilm

Arseny Tarkovsky is considered by many to be one of the prominent Russian poets and translators of the twentieth century. His poetry continued the tradition of the Acmeist poets, a group of Russian transients who wrote poetry predominately before the Bolshevik revolution, including poets Osip Mandelstam and Nikolay Gumilyoy. The most notable poetic figure in his life was the formidable, tragic poet Marina Tsvetaeva who sought a romantic affair with Arseny Tarkovsky some years before her marriage to fellow poet Sergei Efron. After her eventual suicide, Tarkovsky would bear enormous guilt over her death, which he expressed in his delicate, tender poem 'Chistopol Notebook'. Unlike many of his contemporary poets of the era, Tarkovsky was not persecuted his whole career as aggressively by the Soviets—Efron, Gumilyoy, and Mandelstam were all eventually executed by various trumped-up conspiratorial charges—perhaps because Tarkovsky's work was often more abstractly apolitical, poetry that tried to look inward, more concerned with imagined and shared human experience than the contemporary moment. This wasn't always the case though; as a teenager, Tarkovsky and some of his friends wrote an acrostic poem satirizing Lenin and the Chekists. They were arrested and sent in a boxcar to be executed in Mykolaiv, in Ukraine. Tarkovsky managed to take advantage of a moment of distraction and slip away. Every single remaining passenger, all his friends, were killed. Arseny's poetry has not considerably punctured its way into western poetry circles—mostly because it is by nature, quintessentially Russian in character—a language, whose poetry often thrived on the multi-syllabic nature of its word structures, as well as its precise pentameter and irreducible particularities in its line structures. This makes it very difficult to translate, and more so, to do in a way that at all maintains its poetic integrity. Tarkovsky's work can be fulcrum of this translational dilemma. When praising Metres and Psurtsev's 2015 translation, Ukrainian-American poet Ilya Kaminsky spoke on the issues with translating Russian poetry to English, in his blurb for the book:

> How does one translate the work of Russian classic, Arseny Tarkovsky? Imagine trying to translate Yeats: high style rhetoric, intense emotion, local tonalities of language, complicated historical background, the old equation of poet vs. state, the tone of a tender love lyric, all meshed into one, all exquisite in its execution—and all so impossible to render again. And yet, one tries. [...] The gravity and directness of Tarkovsky's tone is brought into English without fail, it is here, honest and pained, piercing and even shy at times, like a deer that looks straight at you before it runs. Tarkovsky's ambition was to seek us—those who live after him—through earth, through time.

The versions of Tarkovsky's poems that appear in his son's films, are often more literal translations, lacking in some of the lush poetic liberties that some of the modern academics have siphoned. Indeed, on translating Tarkovsky's work, Metres notes the main dilemma of the translation process: 'how to demonstrate his near-polyphonic facility for variable patterns of rhythm and sound over the course of how many poems, without flattening that work to a dull iambic or free verse style with some half-hearted gesture toward rhyme?' (xiv). For a novice in poetic translation, this could seem rather overwhelming. Metres and Psurtsev's book does a very good job of balancing the poetic and comprehension of Tarkovsky's poetry. In relation to the films, the balance is careful as well, but the intensity of focus on understanding seems to take priority to the backboard of poetic integrity. Consider this version of the final stanza of the same poem 'And now summer has left' taken from an earlier translation of *Stalker* into English:

> The leaves were not burnt,
> The branches were not broken...
> the day is clean like glass,
> But it is not enough.

Again, similar enough to convey the literal interpretation, but slight differences, sometimes more 'literally' clear, but less-poetically intact.

Andrei Tarkovsky's usage of the poetry of his father in his work is consistent throughout his films. Although *Ivan's Childhood*, his first feature film, does not actually contain any of Arseny Tarkovsky's poems, there is an intriguing thematic continuity with his poem 'Ivan', which is fairly interesting when one considers that Tarkovsky himself did not actually write the film—he was brought onto the existing project. His later films, *The Mirror* and *Stalker* are chalk-full of his father's poems. Tarkovsky never utilizes his father's work with any sort of greed or capitalist incentive for the inclusion; he's not trying to sell any poetry books. He was very firmly raised with his father's poetry, it's as grounding for him as any scriptural text, and of course, the poems are all of a very high-quality in terms of all this working in a succinct way in his films.

Fyodor Tyutchev

In 2008, Icelandic pop-vocalist Björk released her seventh album, *Volta* on One Little Indian Records. It was a successful record and contained one song of notably interesting origins: 'The Dull Flame of Desire'. The song—which also features chilling vocals from the singer Anohni—takes its lyrics from a Russian poem, of the same name, by 19th-century poet Fyodor Tyutchev. When sung by these talented vocalists, the words aberrate with a haunting quality—however, as superb a single as it is, it can't hold a candle to the chilling rendition from *Stalker*, read at the end of the film, by Stalker's Daughter Martiška (played by Natasha Abramova). It is one of several incurrences of poetic influence by Tarkovsky in the film. As well as the work of his father Arseny Tarkovsky, he concludes the film with the poem 'Dull Flame of Desire' by Tyutchev, who Dostoyevsky once allegedly called the greatest Russian poet. Tyutchev was beloved in his time, and still in contemporary Russian poetry he is one of the most studied figures. His poetry was often set to music even before Björk, in the 20th century, by famous Russian composers such as Rachmaninoff and Tchaikovsky.

Tarkovsky uses language brilliantly in *Stalker*, a film with extremely minimal dialogue, like a poem—there's a lot going on in the white space. His decision to end the film with the Tyutchev poem is pointed—the scene in question shows the Stalker's Daughter, who we have barely any interaction with, lying with her head on the table, and then apparently demonstrating telekinetic ability as a climax to the poem; then, the film ends. 'Dull Flame of Desire' is a short love poem:

> I love those eyes of yours, my friend,
> Their sparkling, flashing, fiery wonder;
> When suddenly those lids ascend,
> Then lightning rips the sky asunder;
> You swiftly glance, and there's an end;
> There's greater charm, though, to admire
> When lowered are those eyes divine
> In moments kissed by passion's fire;
> When through the downcast lashes shine
> The smoldering embers of desire...

Monkey outside the bar. © Mosfilm

Tyutchev's poetry was prototypical modernism, anxious, yet firm. His poems—especially the love poems—are laced with contradiction, a polytonality that reaches for personal affirmation in the romance as well as something greater. Tarkovsky ends *Stalker* with these words, and the Stalker's daughter sliding the glass wordlessly across the table. It's leisurely, ominous but perhaps because of the loving content of the poem, there is a sense of hopefulness, rarely present in much of the film, the implication that perhaps the Stalker's daughter will not live the same kind of gloomy pointless existence he has.

Tyutchev's poem is another good example of the interesting choices in translation made by the various versions of the film throughout the years, as well as varieties of the poem translated in collections. Björk's version arguably lacks some of the poetic and winsome language featured in the film: 'ascend' and 'asunder' are replaced by the more literal, direct translations 'rise' and 'everywhere' respectively, which speak to the difference in intent; Björk is going for the jugular, an affect of the overall episteme of the poem, whereas the Tarkovsky incantation seems more rigidly unique. In his standard fashion, it is slightly devoid in its own language, of whatever religious intent, instead content to float individualistically as a new poem.

Endnotes

18. An important distinction should be made early on between the two terms here: 'poetics of cinema' and 'poetic cinema' the latter, a subgenre of films; often lethargic with surrealist or Dada undertones—nonsensical at times, think films like *The Color of Pomegranates*, *The Trilogy of Life* (1971-1974), or *Gummo* (1997). I don't think Tarkovsky would necessarily react so violently to praise of his use of poetry in his films which is frequent and tasteful, as well as the poetic quality of his films, which is of the highest caliber.
19. This is just one translation of the poem—as it appears in *I Burned at the Feast: Selected Poems of Arseny Tarkovsky* translated by Philip Metres and Dimitri Psurtsev, published in 2015. It is a firm and clear translation but to note the distinct difficulty of translating Cyrillic note this translation by Kitty Hunter-Blair's translation of the last stanza of the poem, as featured in the English version of Tarkovsky's book *Time Within Time*: 'Not a leaf was burnt up / Not a twig ever snapped. . ./ Clean as a glass is the day / But there has to be more.' The message is the same, but the language choices are clearly subjective.

Afterword

'Let everything that's been planned come true. Let them believe. And let them have a laugh at their passions. Because what they call passion actually is not some emotional energy, but just the friction between their souls and the outside world. And most important, let them believe in themselves.' – Stalker's Prayer (*Stalker*, 1979)

© *Daisy Braun*

The return to the bar after our time in the Room is startling. Dreamily, we have traveled with these men so far, really for only a relatively short period of time, but devastatingly inexhaustible in its emotional, spiritual, and philosophical varieties. The men are denied a miracle, they sit in silence until Stalker departs with his family. While he lies in his bed, the miracle occurs in the ordinate setting of the Soviet apartment. And with *Ode to Joy* reverberating, colliding with the vibrations of a train in the distance, the film comes to its end. Like Dostoyevsky for Russian literature, Tarkovsky has succeeded with an almost unachievable feat; creating art that which—borrowing from poet Wallace Stevens—achieves the most difficult task; when in the presence of the extraordinary actuality, *a consciousness* taking the place of imagination. In one shot of *Stalker* in the Zone we can see submerged in the water a card from a calendar with the date 28 December, likely chosen innocuously. Years later, it would be this day that Tarkovsky's life would end, and additionally, it is speculated on that he, and others died *because* of filming *Stalker*: Anatoly Solonitsyn (who portrayed the Writer) and Larisa Tarkovskaya (Assistant Director for *Stalker* and Tarkovsky's wife) both died from lung cancer, not far afield from Tarkovsky himself who died from pneumonia brought on by cancer of the bronchial tubes. When filming *Stalker*, they spent a lot of time shooting downstream from a chemical plant, which poured out poisonous liquids into the waters. There's some grand filmic irony to all of this. Tarkovsky was so insistently against the mysticism of his science-fiction film, and wanted the Zone not construed as some grand metaphor of philosophical implications. He wanted it to be a backdrop, just this defined place. Then in the end, creating it likely resulted in his death, rendering it forever *especially* significant. This said: It all comes down to faith, faith of all forms, which given the faith-heavy themes of this film, is appropriate. Since you cannot adequately produce an imagined formulation of deepest desire, the Room is incapable of fulfilling it, but still, grants a diluted desire. At the end of the day, the constructed space leaves us with no deliberate answer.

So very few films convey such a delicate interconnection of personal journey, of philosophy and spirituality, and of illuminating the lived word, the natural one, as well as the world of dreams and imagination, the science-fiction. *Stalker* is one of these films, likely the best, to achieve all of this, and magnificently. The reach of *Stalker* is endless—the film is as topical and relevant more than 40 years later as it must have been in the theatre in its premiere. And Tarkovsky, as influential as ever. Perhaps the subtext feels different; the importance of nature in the absence of humanity feels very relatable with Global Warming on our minds; the shadows of a possibly fascistic military on the edges of the film feels more weighted now than before. The nuclear winter of the Cold War is no longer, but certainly the fear and trembling remain. The Anthropocene dividend continues to toll heavily on everyone, in a way that keeps the inexplicably terrifying Zone as terrifying as ever.

Stalker, though, perhaps isn't so encompassed on fear or visions of a nihilistic visions of an authoritarian nuclear future. As Tarkovsky himself has said, it's a film about human dignity, about faith, and grasping anxiously for an attempted grip on the ineffable, the divine. As Tarkovsky also said, the purpose of art must is to harrow the soul in preparation for death. *Stalker* is where he comes closest to this objective.

CONSTELLATIONS

Films Cited

Battleship Potemkin (Sergei Eisenstein, 1925)

The Wizard of Oz (Victor Fleming, 1939)

Rashomon (Akira Kurosawa, 1950)

Throne of Blood (Akira Kurosawa, 1957)

The Seventh Seal (Ingmar Bergman, 1957)

Ivan's Childhood (Andrei Tarkovsky, 1962)

Shadows of Forgotten Ancestors (Sergei Parajanov, 1965)

Andrei Rublev (Andrei Tarkovsky, 1966)

The Color of Pomegranates (Sergei Parajanov, 1965)

Solaris (Andrei Tarkovsky, 1972)

Jeanne Dielman, 23 quai du Commerce, 1080 Bruxelles (Chantal Akerman, 1975)

Stalker (Andrei Tarkovsky, 1979)

Raiders of the Lost Ark (Steven Spielberg, 1981)

Nostalghia (Andrei Tarkovsky, 1983)

Andrei Tarkovsky & Sergei Parajanov: Islands (Levon Grigoryan, 1988)

Three Colors Trilogy (Krzystof Kieslowski, 1993–1994)

Cube (Vincenzo Natali, 1997)

The Matrix (The Wachowskis, 1999)

There Will Be Blood (Paul Thomas Anderson, 2007)

Antichrist (Lars Von Trier, 2009)

Looper (Rian Johnson, 2012)

The Killing of a Sacred Deer (Yorgos Lanthimos, 2017)

Westworld (HBO, Jonathan Nolan, 2017–)

Stalker Criterion Collection DVD (2017) Special Features:
   - Interview with Rashit Safullin (unknown date)
   - Interview with Eduard Artemyev (2000)
   - Interview with Geoff Dyer (2017)

Bibliography

Roadside Picnic: Introduction

Bereś Stanisław. *Conversations with Stanislaw Lem*. Kraków, Poland: Wydawnictwo Literackie, 1987.

Dyer, Geoff. *Zona: A Book about a Film about a Journey to a Room*. Edinburgh, Scotland: Canongate Books Ltd, 2013. p. 13.

Iho, Arvo. *Painted With Light*. trans. Liis Kolle and Einde O'Callaghan, Tallinn, Estonia: Kultuuripealinn, 5 August, 2011.

Johnson, Vida T., and Graham Petrie. *Tarkovsky: A Visual Fugue*. Bloomington, IN: Indiana University Press, 1994.

Le Guin, Ursula. 'A New Book by the Strugatskys' *Science Fiction Studies*, Vol. 4, No. 12, Greencastle, IN: Depauw University, July, 1977.

Maslin, Janet. ''Stalker' Russian Science-Fiction', Review of *Stalker*, The New York Times, 20 Oct. 1982, p. 23.

Tarkovsky, Andrei. *Sculpting in Time: Reflections on the Cinema*. trans. Kitty Hunter Blair, Austin, TX: University of Texas Press, 2012. pp. 181, 192-193.

---. *Time Within Time: the Diaries, 1970-1986*. trans. Kitty Hunter Blair, London, UK: Faber & Faber, 1994. pp. 66, 101, 146, 152, 174, 250.

Tetsuro, Mayuzumi. 'Kurosawa: "Tarkovsky Was a Real Poet"'. trans. Sato Kimitoshi, Osaka, Japan: *Asahi Shimbun Newspaper*, Nostalghia.com. April 15, 1987.

I. Pliancy and Weakness (Character Examinations)

Brežná, Irena. 'An Enemy of Symbolism'. *Andrei Tarkovsky: Interviews*, ed. John Gianvito, Jackson, MS: U.P. of Mississippi, 2006, pp. 106–123.

LeClair, Anthony V. 'Tarkovsky's *Nostalghia*: Beauty in Maddeningly Antifeminist Visual Poetry'. *Cinapse*, January 22, 2014.

Pua, Phoebe 'Compositions of Crisis: Sound and Silence in the Films of Bergman and Tarkovsky'. Acton, Australia: Australian National University, 2014. p. 68.

Sontag, Susan. 'The Decay of Cinema'. *The New York Times*, 25 Feb. 1996.

Tarkovsky, *Sculpting in Time*. pp. 199-200.

II. Inside the Zone

Bird, Robert. *Andrei Tarkovsky: Elements of Cinema*. London: Reaktion Books, 2008. pp. 68-69.

Capo, Luisa 'Interview with Tarkovsky' *Scena*, Achab. No. 4, 1980. pp. 119-127.

Cosse, Laurence. 'Portrait of a Filmmaker as a Monk-Poet', ed. Gianvito, *Interviews*, p. 169.

Deleuze, Gilles. *Cinema 2: The Time-Image*. trans. Hugh Tomlinson and Robert Galeta, Minneapolis, MN: University of Minnesota Press, 1989. pp. 42-43.

Derrida, Jacques. *Right of Inspection*. trans. David Wills, New York: Monacelli Press, April 1, 1998.

Hjelmgaard, Kim 'Why a babushka in Chernobyl's Exclusion Zone refuses to leave home'. Mclean, VA: *USA Today*. April 17, 2016.

Montgomery, Jesse. 'What Is the Zone and Are We in It? Visions of the Anthropocene in Andrei Tarkovsky's *Stalker*'. Nashville, TN: Vanderbilt University, 2015. p. 43.

Riley, John A. 'Hauntology, Ruins, and the Failure of the Future in Andrei Tarkovsky's *Stalker*'. *Journal of Film and Video*, Volume 69, No. 1, Champaign, IL: University of Illinois Press. 2017. p. 20.

Tarkovsky, *Time Within Time*. p. 159.

Tassone, Aldo. 'Interview with Andrei Tarkovsky (on *Stalker*)', ed. Gianvito, *Interviews*, p. 55.

Turchiano, Danielle. 'Lisa Breaks Down Directing "Westworld"'. New York: *Variety*, 13 May 2018.

Žižek, Slavoj. 'The Thing From Inner Space: On Tarkovsky'. *Angelaki: Journal of the Theoretical Humanities*, Abingdon, UK: Routledge. 1999. pp. 221-231.

III. The Aesthetics of *Stalker*

Adorno, Theodor W. *Aesthetic Theory*. trans. Robert Hullot-Kentor, University of Minnesota Press, 1998. p. 19.

Benjamin, Walter. 'The Work of Art in the Age of Mechanical Reproduction'. *Illuminations*. trans. Harry Zohn. New York: Schoken Books, 2007. p. 234.

Deleuze, *Cinema 2*. p. 73.

Iho, Arvo. *Painted With Light*.

Strick, Philip. 'Tarkovsky's Translations', ed. Gianvito, *Interviews*. p. 72.

Tarkovsky, Andrei. *Sculpting in Time*. pp. 138, 159-162.

Tarkovsky, *Time Within Time*. p. 356.

    (NOTE: an interview with Maria Chuganova entitled 'On Cinema, 1966).

Turovskaya, Maya. *7½ Films of Andrei Tarkovsky*. trans. Richard Taylor, Izd-Vol 'Iskusstvo', London: Faber & Faber, 1991. Archived on Nostalghia.com

IV. The Poetics of *Stalker* (Poetic Cinema)

Batuman, Elif. 'Sergei Paradjanov: film-maker of outrageous imagination'. London: *The Guardian*, 12 March, 2010.

Björk. 'The Dull Flame of Desire'. Words by Fyodor Tyutchev, Music by Björk Guðmundsdóttir. *Volta*, London: One Little Independent. 1 May 2007.

Ciment, Michel, et, al. 'The Artist in Ancient Russia and in the New USSR'. ed. Gianvito, *Interviews*, p. 21.

Christie, Ian. 'Against Interpretation: An Interview with Andrei Tarkovsky'. ed. Gianvito, *Interviews*, p. 69.

Sontag, Susan. 'The Aesthetics of Silence'. *Styles of Radical Will*. New York: Farrar, Straus and Giroux, 1969. pp. 6-7.

Tarkovsky, Andrei. *Sculpting in Time*. pp. 68-69.

Tarkovsky, Arseny. *I Burned at the Feast: Selected Poems of Arseny Tarkovsky*. trans. Philip Metres and Dimitri Psurtev, Cleveland, OH: Cleveland State University Poetry Center, 2015. p. xiv.

Tonino, Guerra. '*Stalker*: Smuggler of Happiness'. ed. Gianvito, *Interviews*, pp. 53-54.

Constellations

'This stunning, sharp series of books fills a real need for authoritative, compact studies of key science fiction films. ...the volumes in the Constellations series promise to set the standard for SF film studies in the 21st century.' Wheeler Winston Dixon, Ryan Professor of Film Studies, University of Nebraska

Children of Men – Dan Dinello

"...an impressive, intelligent and perceptive analysis of a film increasingly recognised in retrospect as a classic of modern dystopian cinema." Starburst

Close Encounters of the Third Kind – Jon Towlson

"...a thoroughly researched, lucid, and insightful study that succeeds on multiple levels of inquiry." Extrapolation

Ex Machina – Joshua Grimm

Exploring Ex Machina's ideas about consciousness, embodiment, and masculinity, all through the lens of a misogynist mad scientist, Joshua Grimm argues the result is a fascinating and unique film that immediately established Alex Garland as a breakout voice in the landscape of science fiction film.

Robocop – Omar Ahmed

"...this exceptional monograph... is essential reading for sf and film critics as well as fans who are nostalgic for an era that marked the end of sf as a genuine art form." Extrapolation